THE GATEWAY EXPERIENCE

Lessons in Manifesting, Astral Travel, Developing ESP, & More

The Complete Guide to the
Declassified Document &
Hemi-Sync Audio Program

D. M. PALMER

THE
GATEWAY
EXPERIENCE

Lessons in Manifesting, Astral Travel,
Developing ESP, & More

The Complete Guide to the
Declassified Document &
Hemi-Sync® Audio Program

D. M. PALMER

THE GATEWAY EXPERIENCE
LESSONS IN MANIFESTING, ASTRAL TRAVEL, DEVELOPING ESP, & MORE

The Complete Guide to the Declassified Document
& Hemi-Sync Audio Program

DESIREE M. PALMER

ISBN 978-1-7373455-5-8

Dedication

To the mystery of the unknown
and the allure of secrets.
To the valiant pursuers of truth.
To the steadfast believers and tireless seekers.
To the trailblazing pioneers
and passionate educators.
To the souls embarked on their journeys
and those yet to begin.
This is for us all!

CONTENTS

ORIGINATION 1

In the beginning. 3

Overview of The CIA Document 7

1. Introduction 9

2. Hypnosis 15

3. Transcendental Meditation 21

4. Biofeedback 25

5. Gateway and Hemi-Sync® 29

6. Lamp vs. Laser 35

7. Frequency Following Response 39

8. Role of Resonance 43

9. Brain Stimulation 47

10. Energy Entrainment 51

11. Consciousness and Energy 55

12. Holograms 59

13. The Part Encodes the Whole 63

14. The Consciousness Matrix 65

15. Brain in Phase 71

16. Evaluation 77

17. Self-Cognition 81

18. Time-Space Dimension 85

19. Intervening Dimensions 91

20. Subatomic Particles 97

21. Dimensions In-between 101

22. Special Status, OBE 105

23. Absolute in Perspective 109

24. From Big Bang to Torus 113

25. Our Place in Time 119

26. Quality of Consciousness 123

27. Consciousness in Perspective 127

28. Gateway Method 131

29. Hemi-Sync® Introduced 137

30. Advanced Techniques 141

31. The Out-of-Body Movement 157

32. Role of REM Sleep 161

33. Information Collection Potential 165

34. Belief System Considerations 169

35. Left brain limitations. 172

36. Self-knowledge. 173

37. Motivational Aspect 177

38. Conclusion 181

Overview of the Hemi-Sync® Audios 185

Focus Levels Explained 191

How to Listen 209

Wave I: Discovery 215

Discovery #1: Orientation 219

Discovery #2: Introduction to Focus 10 229

Discovery #3: Advanced Focus 10........................233

Discovery #4: Release and Recharge 241

Discovery #5: Exploration Sleep...........................245

Discovery #6: Free Flow 10 249

Wave II: Threshold 257

Threshold #1: Introduction to Focus 12 259

Threshold #2: Problem Solving 261

Threshold #3: One-Month Patterning 263

Threshold #4: Color Breathing 269

Threshold #5: Energy Bar Tool (EBT)..................271

Threshold #6: Living Body Map (LBM) 275

Wave III: Freedom..281

Freedom #1: Liftoff 291

Freedom #2: Remote Viewing 293

Freedom #3: Vectors..299

Freedom #4: Five Questions 301

Freedom #5: Energy Food......................................303

Freedom #6: First-Stage Separation....................305

Wave IV: Adventure...313

Adventure #1: One Year Patterning 315

Adventure #2: Five Messages 319

Adventure #3: Free Flow 12 321

Adventure #4: Non-Verbal Communication........323

Adventure #5: NVC II 325

Adventure #6: ComPoint 327

Wave V: Exploring 329

Exploring #1: Advanced Focus 12 333

Exploring #2: Discovering Intuition 335

Exploring #3: Exploring Intuition 337

Exploring #4: Intro to Focus 15 339

Exploring #5: Mission 15 341

Exploring #6: Exploring Focus 15 343

Wave VI: Odyssey 347

Odyssey #1: Sensing 351

Odyssey #2: Expansion 353

Odyssey #3: Point of Departure 355

Odyssey #4: Nonphysical Friends 357

Odyssey #5: Intro to Focus 21 361

Odyssey #6: Free Flow Focus 21 363

Wave VII: Voyager 365

Voyager #1: Explore Total Self 367

Voyager #2: Intro to Focus 23 369

Voyager #3: Intro to Focus 25 371

Voyager #4: Intro to Focus 27 373

Voyager #5: Retrieval 375

Voyager #6: Messages from Beyond 379

Encoding Instructions 381

Trouble Shooting 387

Congratulations! 405

Sources 409

    As Listed in the Original CIA Document 409

    Additional Sources Sited 410

    Table of Abbreviations 411

ORIGINATION

Welcome to a realm where truth and secrets intertwine, where the boundaries of reality and the extraordinary blur into one captivating tapestry. Within these pages, you will find enigmatic knowledge that is not fiction. Prepare to embark on a journey that will challenge your perceptions and unlock the dormant potential of your mind.

At the heart of this book lies a document, shrouded in secrecy, now accessible on CIA.gov through the Freedom of Information Act Electronic Reading Room. Once highly classified, the Gateway Process has emerged from the shadows, now available for all to explore. As you delve into this intriguing world, you will discover that humanity's understanding of its own mental capabilities is but a fraction of what lies dormant within us. Astonishing phenomena like telekinesis, astral projection, and mind-matter manipulation are not mere figments of imagination;

they are part of our innate potential waiting to be harnessed.

To unravel the mysteries of the Gateway Process, we will examine the remarkable training techniques employed by government operatives, allowing them to "spy" from the confines of their offices. Central to this training is a proprietary audio program known as Hemi-Sync®, crafted by the visionary Robert Monroe, founder of the Monroe Institute. The Gateway Journey training awaits those who dare to step into the unknown and explore the uncharted territories of their consciousness.

This book is not a mere retelling of personal experiences or fantastical tales. No, it is a detailed exploration of the process itself, designed for those eager to comprehend the Gateway Experience and delve deeper into its transformative power. As we journey together, we will not only uncover the depths of the Hemi-Sync® audios but also unveil the profound experiences of participants who have undergone this extraordinary training.

It is crucial to approach this exploration with an open mind and an awareness of the cautionary tales that accompany it. The very same minds that once sought to control others through the infamous MK-Ultra program may have played a role in developing the Gateway Process. Yet, as we tread carefully through history's shadowed corridors, we can grasp the potential for genuine enlightenment and a deeper connection with the energy that shapes our existence.

So, dear reader, are you prepared to unlock the mysteries within yourself? As we delve into transcendental meditation, quantum physics, and the wisdom of both Eastern and Western traditions, be prepared for revelations that will forever change your perspective on the human mind. The journey ahead is both captivating and treacherous, but together, we will chart a course into the realms of truth and revelation. Let us embrace the enigma that lies before us, for our quest for knowledge and self-discovery begins now.

In the beginning.

This CIA released document begins with McDonnell presenting a summary page to his commander, explaining his task of assessing The Gateway Experience regarding its mechanics and potential for practical implementation. To ensure accuracy, he recognized the need for extensive research to fully comprehend the process. In his investigation, McDonnell not only explored the biomechanical aspects but also delved into quantum mechanics, aiming to explain the workings of human consciousness and its interaction with the Hemi-Sync® audios. At the core of The Gateway Experience lies a brain hemisphere synchronization process, which demands better understanding.

While some may find this explanation tedious or unnecessary, I believe you will find it immensely helpful in bridging the intellectual gap between reality and the supernatural. McDonnell was concerned that the methods and practices involved might perceived as too "occult" and not recognized as legitimate scientific studies. Consequently, he chose to adopt physics as the most fitting approach to explain The Gateway Process phenomenon.

Understanding the physics behind an altered state of human consciousness involves grappling with concepts that may not be easily grasped or visualized by typical left-brain thinkers. These concepts are non-linear and require the engagement of the creative and intuitive right brain for a comprehensive understanding.

One of McDonnell's significant points in his introduction is a reminder that this process, its understanding, practice, and potential acceptance, should not offend traditional mindsets, religions, or values. He acknowledged the truth that society tends to reject foreign ideas, even if they feel more truthful than false. In his approach, he aimed to open the minds of readers to embrace something new and different, allowing for the analysis to be read and comprehended rather than immediately rejected.

McDonnell went on to explain that "USAINSCOM personnel [...] are required to take the Gateway training or work with Gateway materials," indicating that this process is not only utilized within the US Army Intelligence and Security Command but is also mandatory.

To avoid confusion, it is crucial to understand the distinction between the Hemi-Sync® audios and The Gateway Process itself. The Monroe Institute sells the Hemi-Sync® audios, which are utilized in The Gateway Experience Training. While these terms are often used interchangeably, it is important to note that Hemi-Sync® serves as an audio aid employed within a training program called The Gateway Experience (also known as The Gateway Process and The Gateway Journey).

As we explore this document, we will follow this format: I will share a brief overview of what McDonald intended to convey in the section, followed by a re-written section of the document (to offer more clarity), and then a summary and any additional information that I find helpful to fully grasping the section.

I will do this for each section of the document, as reading the document itself has proven to be a difficult task for some. Nonetheless, the document is available on-line for those who wish to read it directly and make their own interpretations. Please keep in mind page 25 is missing online. Through research it has been located and is included in this summary.

So, let's get started!

Overview of The CIA Document

1. Introduction

The Monroe Institute's technique for achieving altered states of consciousness, known as The Gateway Experience, involves brain hemisphere synchronization, or "Hemi-Sync®." To grasp the process fully, it is essential to have a basic understanding of some bio functional methods employed, such as hypnosis, transcendental meditation, and biofeedback. While these techniques share certain common aspects with The Gateway Experience, they remain distinct. This understanding provides a useful and scientifically accepted foundation for delving deeper into the process.

Furthermore, there is a complete seven "wave" course of audios called Hemi-Sync® available through The

Monroe Institute. This auditory class requires the use of a headset capable of delivering left and right channel sound. Specific sound waves are sent to your left ear, while other waves are sent to your right ear. The purpose of this training is to achieve a heightened level of consciousness. Completing this course is said to enable individuals to perform remarkable feats, such as time travel, remote viewing, and inducing self-induced states of Kundalini bliss.

The original CIA document, though in the public domain, has been carefully edited and revised in this book to enhance clarity and understanding. The intention is to preserve the original authors' message while improving your grasp of the discussions and explanations. Additionally, by providing an overview of the complete Gateway audios, this book equips you to make an informed decision about investing your time and resources in The Gateway Experience. It also prepares you to embark on the training sessions if you choose to do so.

This journey offers a transformative experience for those who wish to explore natural states of altered consciousness, develop unique metaphysical talents, engage in self-healing, and attain a profound understanding of both them and the world around them. Additionally, this retelling demonstrates that you have the capacity to align your mind independently, without external influence.

Regardless of your choice—whether to undergo the training, venture solo, or take no action—upon completing this book, you will possess a deeper comprehension of the CIA document and the Monroe

Institute's role in training Government agents in the realm of Extra Sensory Skills.

Our journey begins with the original author's introduction of the document to the US Army Operational Group Command, to whom he tailored the report.

****

You tasked me with evaluating The Gateway Experience in terms of mechanics and ultimate practicality. As I embarked on this mission, it became evident that to assess the validity and practicality of the process, thorough research and analysis were essential to fully comprehend how and why it operates. I must admit, sir, that this undertaking proved to be intricate and challenging. Initially, I relied on Itzhak Bentov's biomedical models, drawing information about the physical aspects of the process from conversations with a physician who underwent the Gateway training alongside me. However, I soon realized that I needed to delve into various sources on quantum mechanics to elucidate the nature and functioning of human consciousness. I sought to construct a scientifically sound and reasonably clear model of how consciousness functions under Monroe's brain hemisphere synchronization technique. Subsequently, I turned to theoretical physics to explain the nature of the time-space dimension and how expanded human consciousness surpasses it to achieve the goals of the Gateway. Lastly, I recognized the necessity of employing physics to describe the entire phenomenon of out-of-body states within the language of physical science, eradicating the stigma of occult associations and rendering it amenable to objective assessment.

To start the narrative, I briefly profiled the fundamental biomedical factors influencing related techniques like hypnosis, biofeedback, and transcendental meditation. This comparison aimed to aid the reader in comprehending the Gateway experience as the model of its underlying mechanics was developed. Additionally, the introductory material lends support to the conclusions of this paper. I posit that these related techniques might offer useful entry points for facilitating entry into the Gateway Experience on occasion.

The esteemed physicist Niels Bohr once responded to his son's complaints about the complexity of certain physics concepts by saying, "You are not thinking, you are merely being logical." The physics of altered human consciousness involves concepts that are challenging to grasp or visualize within the confines of traditional "left-brain" linear thinking. Borrowing Dr. Bohr's phrase, some parts of this paper will demand not only logic but also a touch of right-brain intuitive insight to achieve a complete and comfortable understanding of the involved concepts. Nevertheless, once achieved, I am confident that their design and implementation will withstand rational scrutiny.

After making extensive efforts to avoid judgment based on an occult or dogmatic framework, I felt compelled to briefly address the impact of The Gateway Experience on common belief systems. While it was crucial to refrain from assessing

*the concept within such systems, I sensed
it necessary, upon completing the analysis,
to emphasize that the resulting conclusions
do not contradict the fundamental tenets of
either eastern or western belief systems.
Unless this point is clearly established,
there is a risk that some individuals may
reject the entire concept of The Gateway
Experience, believing it to be at odds with
what they hold to be right and true.*

*I wish to clarify that this study is not
intended to be the final word on the
subject. However, I hope that the validity
of its basic structure and fundamental
concepts will render it a useful guide for
other USAINSCOM personnel who are required
to undergo Gateway training or work with
Gateway materials.*

Wayne M. McDonnell

LTC, MI Commander, Det 0

2. Hypnosis

The first biomechanical process under review is hypnosis. Hypnosis has been employed for a variety of purposes, including helping individuals overcome undesirable habits and behaviors. Additionally, it has been used for entertainment in comedy clubs and, unfortunately, even for more dubious and manipulative intentions like mind control. Despite this range of uses, hypnosis is widely recognized as a legitimate psychological treatment. McDonnell's aim was to ensure that the reader grasps the biological effects of hypnosis on the mind and body, emphasizing the scientific aspect over fiction.

ORIGINAL CIA REPORT SUMMARY AND OVERVIEW:

Following a successful disengagement of the stimulus screening function of the left brain, hypnosis enables direct access to various areas in the right brain, such as the sensory-motor cortex, pleasure centers, and lower cerebral or emotional regions.

The left hemisphere of the brain operates in a self-cognitive, verbal, and linear manner. It screens incoming stimuli by categorizing, assessing, and attributing meaning before allowing them to enter the right hemisphere. On the other hand, the right hemisphere functions in a noncritical, holistic, nonverbal, and pattern-oriented way, readily accepting what the left hemisphere passes on without questioning.

When the left hemisphere is distracted by external stimuli, hypnotic suggestions can pass into the right hemisphere and be directly accepted and acted upon. These external stimuli may include semi-sleep states, visual interruptions, and auditory cues. The outcome of this process may involve an emotional reaction linked to the newly accessed lower cerebral region or a sensory/motor response involving the cortex. Both the sensory and motor portions of the right brain contain a sequence of points known as the "homunculus," corresponding to specific points in the body (see Exhibit 1, taken from the CIA Document).

Stimulating these processing points leads to mild physical responses in the corresponding parts of the body. For instance, introducing the suggestion to the right brain that a person's legs are numb without the filter of the left brain would remain unchallenged when introduced to the sensory cortex. As a result, an electrical reaction would be generated, inducing the feeling of numbness in the legs. This principle applies to both perceived positive and negative suggestions. Thus,

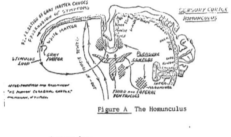

Figure A The Homunculus

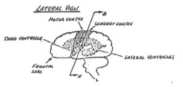

Figure B The Motor and Sensory Cortex and the Third and Lateral Ventricles

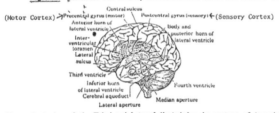

Figure C A view of the Third and Lateral Ventricles in context of Associated Brain Structure.

while in a hypnotic state, a suggestion that the person is experiencing happiness and well-being would target the pleasure centers located in the lower cerebral portion of the cortex, inducing the suggested feeling of euphoria.

In the context of The Gateway Process, this understanding is applied through suggestions that the hypnotic subject possesses enhanced concentration or extraordinary memory. Such suggestions allow access to previously unused information storage, typically restricted due to the left hemisphere's selection and control processes. During the initial stages of the Gateway process, hypnosis can be employed to accelerate progress.

SUMMARY AND ADDITIONS:

When attempting to form new habits, change behaviors, or embrace new concepts, our brains may instinctively resist putting up a stop sign of sorts. Our brain's design aims to protect us and guide us in a unified direction as a species. This evolutionary mechanism has served us well and will continue to do so. However, it also means that when we are predisposed to harmful activities like smoking, alcohol abuse, or overeating of poor-quality foods, we may have limited control to change these behaviors.

Hypnosis practitioners have undergone training to counteract the natural reactions of our left brain, which seeks to shield us from potential harm caused by ourselves. By accessing the right brain and introducing innovative ideas and habits, we increase the likelihood of achieving successful outcomes.

Similarly, if we have distressing memories or experiences that seem entrenched, we may need to

18

overcome the left brain's resistance, acting like a military force against altering our perceptions. In such cases, hypnosis, with the assistance of a trained professional, can help resolve or mitigate the lingering impact of these events.

Essentially, hypnosis involves finding a way to engage or disengage the protective left brain through our senses, so it remains undisturbed while we access the right brain to implant suggestions, remove harmful memories, or cultivate new habits on the right side of the brain.

Included is an easier to see diagram of the Homunculus. Describing that the front cortex controls the motor function and the rear cortex the sensory function.

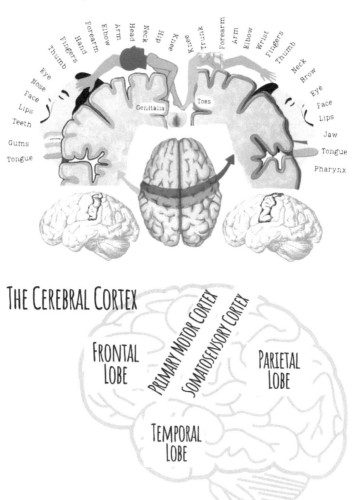

THE CEREBRAL CORTEX

FRONTAL LOBE

PRIMARY MOTOR CORTEX

SOMATOSENSORY CORTEX

PARIETAL LOBE

TEMPORAL LOBE

3. Transcendental Meditation

For over 3,000 years, a trance-like meditative state has been practiced, primarily utilized in spiritual and transcendental movements to enable practitioners to experience the blissful state known as Kundalini. This experience is described in various ways by different individuals, but it typically involves a sense of awakening within the body.

During this practice, many report feeling a wave of energy vibrating and moving through their system, starting from the root chakra (located near the base of the spine) or the area that touches the chair when sitting, and ascending to the top of the head. The sensation is often likened to a sexual orgasm but differs in that it is not localized to the genital area; instead, it permeates the entire body, sometimes even reaching the feet and hands of the participants.

ORIGINAL CIA REPORT SUMMARY AND OVERVIEW:

Transcendental meditation involves a distinct form of hypnosis, characterized by intense and prolonged single-minded concentration on drawing energy up the spinal cord. This process leads to the creation of aural standing waves in the cerebral ventricles, which are then transferred to the gray matter in the cerebral cortex on the right side of the brain. This circuit operates similarly to the brain's heartbeat, stimulating and polarizing the cortex and sending a signal up along the spinal cord towards the brain.

According to the Bentov biomedical model, as described in the book "Kundalini-Psychosis or Transcendence" by Lee Sannella, MD, the standing acoustic waves result from altered heart sound rhythms caused by extended meditation practice. These altered rhythms set up sympathetic vibrations in the walls of the fluid-filled cavities that form the third and lateral ventricles of the brain, creating a memory pathway towards this altered state of mind.

Individuals who have experienced or are in a state of Kundalini bliss describe the state of being as completing a full loop around the hemispheres and back to the lower spine, forming a loop channel. This process can be thought of as "self-

stimulation of the pleasure centers in the brain caused by the circulation of a 'current' along the sensory cortex."

Research suggests that many symptoms of Kundalini bliss begin on the left side of the body, indicating that the part of the brain initiating the experience is on the right side. Developing Kundalini typically requires at least five years of intense practice and concentration due to the complex nature of this yoga. Bentov (1989) explains that this cosmic vibration can be positively attained by prolonged exposure to acoustical or mechanical vibrations ranging from 4 to 7 Hertz.

Additionally, another study found that repeated exposure to vibrations, such as those experienced while riding in a car with poor suspension combined with the constant sensation of air conditioning, could trigger a spontaneous physio-Kundalini sequence in susceptible individuals with a sensitive nervous system. This led to the hypothesis that the blissful state could be induced not only through consistent effort in meditation but also through wave patterns of vibration and sensation.

SUMMARY AND ADDITIONS:

Indeed, both hypnosis and transcendental meditation aim to access the right side of a susceptible brain by either external stimulation of the senses or through the person's own internal activity, respectively. In both cases, the left brain's control is released, leading to similar results in terms of accessing specific areas of the brain. However, the way in which they create a physical response, such as the Kundalini bliss, differs significantly.

Transcendental meditation allows the individual to access and induce the blissful state of Kundalini on their own, offering the advantage of self-control over this process. Through this practice, individuals can learn to access and regulate the functions of the right brain, enabling them to rewire their habits and abilities. By employing predetermined suggestions, they can be guided to the right brain during the Kundalini state, further enhancing their capacity for self-control and personal transformation.

Moreover, like hypnosis, the Kundalini state can be induced in a person through external stimulation. By using a vibration of 4-7 Hertz in conjunction with the meditative trance, a person could experience Kundalini without having undergone the prolonged practice required to create the internal channel vibrations that usually result from extended meditation.

Additionally, this process is describing how an experienced meditation state of heart mind coherence channels spinal fluid up through the spinal cord through the brain and back down in a circular motion, creating a feedback loop. When this sensation is complete the state is achieved.

In essence, both hypnosis and transcendental meditation offer distinct pathways to accessing and harnessing the power of the right brain, each with its unique benefits and applications.

4. Biofeedback

Among the methods we have discussed so far, biofeedback stands out as the most involved and distinct in its approach. Unlike other techniques, biofeedback does not ignore or bypass the left brain; instead, it actively involves the left brain to gain access to the right.

In the biofeedback method, individuals are empowered and placed in the driver's seat, as they are directly in control of forcing or effecting the desired changes. This method does not rely solely on the right brain, which is engaged in other techniques to create change once activated. Instead, biofeedback allows individuals to consciously influence and regulate their physiological responses and bodily functions by providing them with real-time feedback on their bodily processes.

Through biofeedback, individuals can monitor various physiological indicators, such as heart rate, skin conductance, muscle tension, or brainwave patterns, and receive immediate feedback on their responses. By learning to interpret and adjust these signals, they can gain control over their bodily functions and responses, which can lead to various therapeutic benefits.

The active involvement of the left brain in the biofeedback process sets it apart from other methods, as it allows individuals to take an active role in achieving their desired outcomes, making it a powerful tool for self-regulation and personal growth.

ORIGINAL CIA REPORT SUMMARY AND OVERVIEW:

Biofeedback is a consciousness-altering technique that uniquely utilizes the left hemisphere's self-cognitive abilities to gain access to specific areas of the right brain, such as the lower cerebral, motor, sensory cortices, and pain or pleasure centers. Unlike hypnosis, which suppresses the left hemisphere, or transcendental meditation, which largely bypasses it, biofeedback teaches the left hemisphere to visualize the desired outcome and recognize the associated feelings linked to successful right hemisphere access.

Special self-monitoring devices, like a digital thermometer, are employed to alert the left brain when the right hemisphere

*successfully accesses the targeted area.
Once this connection is established, the
left brain can repeatedly instruct the
right brain to reinforce and strengthen the
involved pathways, enabling conscious,
demand-driven access to appropriate areas
of the right brain.*

*For instance, if a subject aims to increase
circulation in their left leg to expedite
healing, they can use their left brain to
focus on this goal while closely monitoring
the temperature of the left leg using a
digital thermometer. As progress is
achieved, the thermometer will indicate an
increase in temperature. The subject can
then mentally associate the sensations with
the desired result and reinforce the
process through memory recall, affirmation,
and repetition. This method has shown
success in pain reduction, accelerated
healing, tumor suppression, stimulation of
pleasure centers, and achieving various
specific physiological outcomes.*

*Additionally, biofeedback can expedite the
attainment of deep meditative states,
especially for beginners who lack prior
experience with meditative techniques.
Displaying a subject's brainwave pattern on
a cathode ray tube has been proven as a
laboratory-validated method for guiding
subjects into profoundly relaxed states
associated with advanced meditation,
characterized by a state of calmness and
singular mental focus.*

SUMMARY AND ADDITIONS:

Biofeedback is indeed one of the most challenging
methods, but it has become one of the most taught

and successful techniques in modern practice precisely because the individual is in control. The ability to monitor indicators like brainwaves and temperature changes allows the subject to have real-time feedback, knowing precisely when their thoughts, actions, and sensations on a mental level are producing the desired effects. This empowers them to replicate and duplicate these effects by recreating the exact same feeling in their body.

As with many skills, practice is crucial to achieving proficiency. With biofeedback, individuals can take charge of their own "bio hacking" journey. However, reaching the point where biofeedback induces change can be initially difficult. Working with a knowledgeable practitioner who possesses the proper measuring tools becomes essential to get started effectively.

The challenge lies in finding such experienced practitioners and acquiring the necessary measuring equipment, which can be both difficult to locate and expensive to engage. Nevertheless, for those who invest the effort and resources into biofeedback, the benefits of being in control of their own consciousness-altering process can be incredibly rewarding.

5. Gateway and Hemi-Sync®

The Hemi-Sync® process, developed by Robert Monroe and utilized by The Monroe Institute, is a method of audio-based guidance that helps individuals achieve altered states of consciousness. At its core, it involves a series of specialized sound patterns and meditation instructions that aim to facilitate the listener's access to universal knowledge and transcend their physical existence. By harnessing universal energies, individuals can focus on specific intentions and achieve various altered states of consciousness.

The process is named Hemi-Sync® because it involves the synchronization of brainwave patterns between the left and right hemispheres of the brain. This synchronization is achieved by using binaural beats or other auditory stimuli that differ in frequency and are presented to each ear separately. The brain then processes these auditory signals, creating a third frequency called the binaural beat. This binaural beat aligns the brainwave patterns of both hemispheres, leading to a state of hemispheric coherence and facilitating the alteration of consciousness.

Hemi-Sync® has been found to be helpful in creating altered states of consciousness due to several reasons:

Brainwave Synchronization: The process synchronizes brainwave patterns, inducing specific states of mind associated with creativity, relaxation, and enhanced learning. It can facilitate access to altered states such as expanded awareness, lucid dreaming, and even out-of-body experiences.

Enhanced Focus and Relaxation: The audio guidance aids in achieving a state of focused attention and deep relaxation, making it easier for individuals to enter altered states and explore their inner experiences.

Accessing Universal Energies: By aligning brainwave patterns, Hemi-Sync® helps individuals tap into universal energies, providing a pathway to higher levels of consciousness and deeper understanding.

Improved Learning and Self-Exploration: The process has been used to enhance learning, memory, and problem-solving abilities. It can also aid in exploring one's consciousness and gaining insights into personal growth and self-awareness.

Potentiation of Intentions: Hemi-Sync® can amplify and potentiate the intentions set by the listener during the meditation, allowing them to manifest their desired outcomes more effectively.

The Hemi-Sync® process has been widely used and researched by The Monroe Institute and other organizations, showing promising results in helping individuals explore and access altered states of consciousness. It remains a popular tool for personal development, self-exploration, and expanding the boundaries of human consciousness.

ORIGINAL CIA REPORT SUMMARY AND OVERVIEW:

The core of The Gateway Experience training system revolves around altering and expanding consciousness by increasing the amplitude and frequency of brainwave output between the left and right hemispheres. The ultimate goal is to transcend the physical sphere and break free from the constraints of time and space, granting participants access to various levels of intuitive knowledge within the universe. What sets The Gateway Experience apart from other forms of meditation is its utilization of the Hemi-Sync® technique, defined as a state of consciousness in which the electroencephalogram (EEG) patterns of both hemispheres are simultaneously equal in amplitude and frequency.

Hemi-Sync® may be relatively rare and of short duration in ordinary human consciousness, but through the use of audio techniques developed by Bob Monroe, the founder of The Monroe Institute, it becomes achievable and sustainable. The institute's basic Focus 3 audios can induce and maintain Hemi-Sync®, a state wherein brainwave patterns are synchronized between the left and right hemispheres.

Research conducted by Elmer and Alyce Greene at the Menninger Foundation revealed that subjects with extensive training in Zen meditation could consistently establish Hemi-Sync® at will and sustain it for over 15 minutes. This suggests that, with proper training and practice, individuals can master this state of consciousness.

Dr. Stuart Twemlow, a psychiatrist and research associate of The Monroe Institute, found that the audios in The Gateway Experience encourage the focusing of brain energy into a narrower frequency band. This focused energy is akin to the concept of one-pointedness in yoga, representing a state of single-mindedness in Western terms. As participants progress through the audios beyond Focus 3, there is a gradual increase in brainwave size, indicating a boost in brain energy or power.

In summary, The Gateway Experience employs the Hemi-Sync® technique to achieve synchronized brainwave patterns, leading to altered states of consciousness and expanded awareness. With consistent practice and training, individuals can access and sustain Hemi-Sync®, unlocking a profound potential for exploring their consciousness and tapping into intuitive knowledge within the universe.

SUMMARY AND ADDITIONS:

The Hemi-Sync® program is an audio program that plays corresponding sound waves in each ear separately, with the goal of aligning and heightening your brainwaves on both sides. This brainwave synchronization typically takes years of practice and meditation to achieve. However, by participating in the Gateway Process, your brain can enter this state and energetically align while listening to the Hemi-Sync® sounds. The ultimate goal is for the subject to recognize these sensations and create pathways, enabling them to replicate the desired outcome without the aid of the Hemi-Sync® audios.

6. Lamp vs. Laser

The difference between a mind with and without Hemi-Sync® training can be likened to the contrast between a standard house light bulb and a targeted laser beam. An unfocused mind, like the energy emitted from a light bulb, scatters in all directions without a clear intention, making it susceptible to interference and distractions. On the other hand, a mind in coherence with itself, through Hemi-Sync® training, generates a focused, intentional, and powerful beam of mental clarity that can cut through interference and remain undistracted in its purpose.

ORIGINAL CIA REPORT SUMMARY AND OVERVIEW:

The process of using Hemi-Sync® in The Gateway Experience can be explained through a metaphor. In its natural state, the human mind is likened to an ordinary lamp that emits energy in the form of both heat and light. However, this energy disperses chaotically and incoherently, spreading over a wide but limited area. Like a light bulb casting a dim light everywhere in a small space, the mind's energy lacks focus and depth as it extends further.

When the human mind is focused with Hemi-Sync®, it transforms into a laser beam, producing a disciplined and concentrated stream of mental energy. This stream of energy possesses total frequency and amplitude coherence, akin to a laser beam containing billions of times more concentrated energy than the sun. As a result, the mind becomes more powerful, projecting a stronger and more directed beam over greater distances.

Gateway believes that once the human brain's frequency and amplitude are made coherent, it can begin accelerating both, allowing the mind to resonate at increasingly higher vibrational levels. In this state, the mind can synchronize itself with more sophisticated and rare energy levels present in the universe. Operating at these heightened levels enables the mind to process the received information using the same fundamental matrix employed to make sense of ordinary physical sensory input and derive meaning in a cognitive context.

This meaning is often perceived visually through symbols, but it can also manifest as profound flashes of holistic intuition or scenarios that involve both visual and auditory perceptions. The mechanics of the mind exercising the consciousness function and its ability to achieve meaning in various ways will be explored further in this paper.

SUMMARY AND ADDITIONS:

In its natural state, our minds may exhibit chaotic energy, dispersing in various directions without a clear sense of direction or purpose. However, when our minds are trained with a system like Hemi-Sync®, the energy remains the same, but it becomes more focused and coherent, like a laser rather than a lamp.

Just as a laser concentrates its light into a powerful, directed beam, a trained mind with Hemi-Sync® becomes more intentional and purposeful. The energy is channeled towards a specific point or goal, allowing for greater clarity, concentration, and effectiveness. Instead of bouncing aimlessly, the mind focuses on a single point, making it more efficient and capable of achieving its objectives.

7. Frequency Following Response

Before delving into Frequency Following Response (FFR) as used in Hemi-Sync®, it's important to establish a basic understanding of the standard brain waves themselves. The acronym D T A B G, or "Dee-Tab-Gee," can help remember the different levels of brain waves. These brain waves are categorized based on their frequency, measured in hertz (hz).

Starting at the lowest frequency level is Delta, ranging from 0.5 to 4 hz. Delta waves are commonly observed during deep dreamless sleep, allowing our bodies to undergo self-repair and rejuvenation. Moving up the frequency scale is Theta, ranging from 4 to 8 hz. Theta waves are associated with dreaming, being in a state of autopilot, and the process of learning.

Continuing up the chart, we have Alpha waves, ranging from 8 to 13 hz. Alpha waves are present when we are in a relaxed or recharging state, often associated with calm and meditative moments. Moving further up, we encounter Beta waves, ranging from 13 to 35 hz. Beta waves are associated with activities requiring problem-solving, engagement, and active mental focus.

Finally, at the top of the standard brain wave chart, we have Gamma waves, which operate at 35+ hz. Gamma waves are found during periods of intense concentration, deep learning, and high-level cognitive processing.

ORIGINAL CIA REPORT SUMMARY AND OVERVIEW:

The Hemi-Sync® technique harnesses a phenomenon known as the Frequency Following Response (FFR) to achieve brain hemisphere synchronization. When a subject is exposed to sound frequencies that mimic those associated with specific brainwave patterns, the brain naturally attempts to mirror the same frequency pattern by adjusting its own brainwave output. For instance, if a subject hears sound frequencies approximating brainwave output at the Theta level (related to Dreaming/Autopilot/Learning), their brain will strive to shift from the normal Beta level (linked to Problem solving/Engaging) to the Theta level.

Since Theta frequencies are typically associated with sleep, the subject may transition from a fully awake state to a sleep state (unless consciously resisted) as the brain endeavors to synchronize its wave frequency output with the one presented through the Hemi-Sync® audio. As these brainwave frequencies lie outside the range of sounds the human ear can hear in their pure form, Hemi-Sync® generates them through another phenomenon known as the brain's ability to perceive "beat" frequencies.

When the brain is exposed to one frequency in the left ear that is ten Hertz below another audible frequency played in the right ear, instead of hearing either of the two audible frequencies, the brain perceives the difference between them as the "beat" frequency. Capitalizing on the FFR phenomenon and utilizing "beat" frequencies, the Gateway system employs Hemi-Sync® and other audio techniques to introduce a variety of frequencies that are played at a virtually subliminal, marginally audible level.

The aim is to relax the left hemisphere of the brain, induce a virtual sleep state in the physical body, and promote coherence between the left and right hemispheres, facilitating the production of increasingly higher amplitude and frequency of brainwave output. Bob Monroe's audible and possibly subliminal suggestions accompany the various brainwave frequencies, which are sometimes combined with other sounds like sea surf to mask the specific sound frequencies when needed.

Through this approach, Gateway aims to provide individuals with the tools to consciously change their consciousness over time through repeated use of the audios. By doing so, participants gain access to new levels of information beyond the reach of ordinary consciousness, accessed through intuitive means.

SUMMARY AND ADDITIONS:

The Hemi-Sync® program employs a technique called "beat" frequency to achieve brain hemisphere synchronization. When the two sides of the brain hear a frequency or sound that is not in sync with each other, they try to make sense of it by "hearing" the difference between the two frequencies. The Hemi-Sync® audio intentionally manipulates the frequencies to create the desired wave level that is most beneficial for the exercise and corresponds to the intended brainwave pattern.

As the left brain engages in processing this altered frequency, it allows the right brain to become accessible and receptive to the suggestions embedded in the audio. This synchronization between the two hemispheres creates a state of coherence and alignment, enhancing the brain's ability to enter altered states of consciousness and facilitate a deeper connection to intuitive knowledge and experiences.

8. Role of Resonance

The human heart and vessel structure generate a resonance frequency or vibration with each heartbeat. This inherent vibrational frequency can be influenced and altered to facilitate higher states of being. The Gateway Process utilizes this principle to aid in implementing changes to the body's frequency and consciousness.

By using techniques like Hemi-Sync® and other audio methods, the Gateway Process aims to synchronize the brain hemispheres and guide the mind into altered states of consciousness. During this process, the vibrational frequency of the heart and body can be influenced and elevated, allowing individuals to access different levels of awareness and explore new realms of intuitive knowledge.

Through repeated practice and exposure to the Gateway audios, individuals can learn to entrain their brainwaves and heart's vibrational frequency, gradually attaining higher states of coherence and expanded consciousness. This process opens the door to profound experiences and deeper understanding of one's inner self and the universe around them.

ORIGINAL CIA REPORT SUMMARY AND OVERVIEW:

Brain coherence achieved through beat frequencies delivered via stereo headphones is just one of the reasons why the Gateway system is effective. Another crucial aspect is to attain the physical stillness associated with deep transcendental meditative states, which leads to a complete alteration of the fundamental resonance pattern associated with the sound frequencies produced by the human body.

With long-term practice of yoga, Zen, or transcendental meditation, a change occurs in the sound frequency with which the human heart resonates throughout the entire body. This change in resonance is a result of the removal of what the medical profession refers to as "the bifurcation echo." The bifurcation echo is caused by the interaction of the pressure pulses generated by the heart's pumping action as they travel along the aorta and then rebound back up. This creates an interference pattern that causes irregularities in the sound frequency of the heart's beating.

The Gateway audios achieve a similar goal to meditation by inducing a profoundly relaxed state in the body. As the body relaxes, the bifurcation echo gradually fades away, and the heart reduces the force and frequency of its pumping, leading to a regular, rhythmic sine wave pattern of sound that echoes throughout the body and rises into the head in sustained resonance. This sine wave pattern, when measured with a sensitive instrument, has an amplitude approximately three times greater than the average sound volume produced by the heart in its normal state of operation.

This altered resonance pattern, combined with the brain hemisphere synchronization induced by Hemi-Sync® and other audio techniques, creates a synergistic effect that helps individuals access altered states of consciousness, higher levels of awareness, and intuitive knowledge. The Gateway Process thus offers a powerful tool for personal growth and exploration of the mind's potential.

SUMMARY AND ADDITIONS:

Our heart is more than just an organ that circulates blood in our veins. At the vibrational frequency level, also known as energy, which is not visible but very much present, the heart acts as the center of an orchestra. It generates its own personal resonance that can be changed and felt not only within us but also by those around us. This phenomenon occurs, in part, through the energy and beat of the heart. Just as we can "feel" when someone is anxious or happy, our human ability to understand the resonance of another person is experienced through energy.

Controlling and synchronizing the resonance of this energy takes years of practice and understanding. The Hemi-Sync® Audios play a vital role in this process by helping to control and synchronize these energy patterns, ensuring that the participants can engage in the training at the highest levels. Using beat frequencies and brain hemisphere synchronization, the Gateway Process facilitates the alignment of both mind and heart, allowing individuals to access altered states of consciousness and explore the depths of their own potential. By tapping into this transformative energy, participants can cultivate a greater sense of self-awareness and harmony, not only within themselves but also in their interactions with others and the world around them.

9. Brain Stimulation

In this section, we will delve into the fascinating realm of brain stimulation and its connection to the heart's rhythmic frequency. We will explore how this resonance impacts the brain and the entire body, as well as its potential effects on the earth's energy levels.

ORIGINAL CIA REPORT SUMMARY AND OVERVIEW:

According to Bentov's biomedical model, the resonance generated by the heart's rhythmic frequency plays a vital role as it directly affects the brain. This resulting vibration is transmitted to the brain through the third and left ventricles, which are fluid-filled spaces above the brain stem. As a consequence, the brain experiences an electromagnetic pulse that stimulates it, increasing both the amplitude and frequency of brainwave output. Dr. Twemlow's research on the effects of Hemi-Sync® audios discovered this brainwave enhancement.

Moreover, the brain is enveloped in a protective membrane called the dura, cushioned by a thin layer of fluid between it and the skull. When the coherent resonance produced by the deeply relaxed human heart reaches this fluid layer surrounding the brain, it induces a rhythmic pattern of movement. The brain gently oscillates up and down in a continuous pattern, approximately 0.005 to 0.010 millimeters in magnitude. This movement persists due to the self-reinforcing nature of resonant behavior, despite the low energy requirement.

In this way, the entire body functions as a harmonious vibrational system, transferring energy in the range of 6.8-7.5 Hertz into the earth's ionospheric cavity, which resonates at a similar frequency of about 7-7.5 Hertz. To put it in perspective, this signal created by our body's movement will travel around the entire planet in about one-seventh of a second through the electrostatic field enveloping us, covering a very long wavelength of approximately 40,000 km, almost equal to the earth's perimeter. This long wavelength remains unaffected by obstacles and retains its strength even over vast distances, easily passing through various mediums like metal, concrete, water, and the fields that *compose our bodies. This makes it an ideal conduit for the potential transmission of telepathic signals.*

Consequently, during the Gateway process, as participants experience deep relaxation, a state of profound calmness begins to permeate their nervous systems. This leads to a significant reduction in blood pressure, causing various physical systems, such as the circulatory system and skeleton, to vibrate coherently at 7-7.5 cycles per second. The resulting resonance produces a regular, repetitive sound wave that synchronizes with the earth's electrostatic field.

SUMMARY AND ADDITIONS:

The interconnectedness of the heart's rhythmic frequency and brain stimulation reveals a fascinating aspect of human physiology. The brain responds to the heart's resonance, creating a vibrational field that extends to encompass the entire earth. Although these processes are physically observed within the body, their transmission occurs through energy pathways.

The Gateway process incorporates audios within these energy fields, facilitating the exploration and understanding of these profound connections between our internal rhythms and the broader energy dynamics of the planet. It provides a unique opportunity for participants to engage with their own inner frequencies and align with the larger vibrational tapestry of existence.

10. Energy Entrainment

When a human participant becomes attuned with the surrounding energies, they establish a profound connection, almost becoming one with the energy itself. This deep attunement opens the door for the consciousness of the participant to move beyond the confines of the physical body and interact with other similar energies. This includes the ability to explore different places and connect with other individuals on a profound level.

ORIGINAL CIA REPORT SUMMARY AND OVERVIEW:

The exercises included in the Gateway audios guide the participant to build up their energy field, drawing upon the energy from the earth's field. As the body becomes coherent and harmoniously resonates with its surroundings, it creates a unified energy continuum with the surrounding electrostatic medium. This alignment of the body's energy field with its environment allows the consciousness to extend beyond the physical boundaries and explore the surroundings.

Through this process, the brain is brought into focused coherence at increasingly higher levels of frequency and amplitude, enabling the attunement with corresponding frequencies in the universe for data collection. It also enhances the participant's physical energy levels, eventually leading to the potential for out-of-body experiences. Moreover, by resonating with the earth's electromagnetic sphere, the human body generates a surprisingly powerful carrier wave, facilitating communication between minds attuned to similar frequencies.

SUMMARY AND ADDITIONS:

The Gateway Process opens the door to what may appear as magic or extraordinary abilities to many. Participants can access a realm where astral travel, mind-reading, and glimpses into the future are within reach, as time is perceived as an illusion in this expanded state of consciousness.

These unique abilities are precisely why the CIA employs this technique to train special agents. The advantage of being able to predict their enemies' moves, gather intelligence without physical engagement, and understand an opponent's motives is of immense value and importance. Through the Gateway Process, individuals can tap into their inherent potential and explore the uncharted territories of consciousness and energy, unlocking hidden talents and understanding the interconnectedness of all things.

11. Consciousness and Energy

There exists a common misconception in the lay world regarding the true nature of matter, energy, and consciousness. In reality, everything we perceive to exist is, at its core, an oscillating energy field – an infinite number of complex energy patterns. This is a scientifically proven fact and forms the basis for understanding how resonance and coherence can lead to altered states of consciousness.

ORIGINAL CIA REPORT SUMMARY AND OVERVIEW:

Before we can proceed with our explanation, it is necessary to define the mechanism by which the human mind performs the function known as consciousness, as well as to describe how that consciousness operates to deduce meaning from the stimuli that it receives. To do so, we will first consider the fundamental nature of the material world in which we live to accurately perceive the raw material with which our consciousness must work.

The first point to make is that the terms matter and energy can be misleading when used to describe two distinct states of existence in the physical world as we know it. Indeed, if the term matter is understood to mean a solid substance as opposed to energy, which is understood to mean some kind of force. With this understanding our current definition of matter is entirely misleading. Science now knows that the electrons that spin in the energy field surrounding the nucleus of the atom, as well as the nucleus itself, are nothing more than oscillating energy grids. In the strictest sense of the term, solid matter does not exist. Rather, atomic structure is made up of oscillating energy grids that are surrounded by other oscillating energy grids that orbit at extremely fast speeds. Itzhak Bentov provides the following figures in his book, Stalking The Wild Pendulum.

The energy grid that makes up the nucleus of the atom vibrates at about 1022 Hertz (which means ten followed by twenty-two zeros). An atom oscillates at 1015 Hertz at 70 degrees Fahrenheit. A molecule, which is

made up of many atoms bound together in a
single energy field, vibrates at 109 Hertz.
A living human cell vibrates at about 103
Hertz. The point is that the entire human
being, brain, consciousness, and all, is
nothing more or less than an
extraordinarily complex system of energy
fields, just like the universe that
surrounds us.

The so-called states of matter are
variations in the state of energy, and
human consciousness is a function of the
interaction of energy in two opposing
states (motion vs. rest).

SUMMARY AND ADDITIONS:

The human brain, and perhaps ego as well, has a difficult time understanding the absolute truth that matter, in effect, the human, does not exist. We can feel our skin, we can see each other's physical being, we can experience the "boundaries" of the physical world. To then say that is all untrue, is hard to comprehend.

Nonetheless, the more we understand that we are oscillating energetic fields, the better we will become at understanding our ability to interact and affect each other with or without our intention to do so.

In The Gateway Process, we embrace this universal truth and work with intention and purpose to explore and unlock hidden knowledge within these intricate energy patterns. Understanding the fundamental nature of consciousness and energy empowers us to engage with the universe in ways that transcend our traditional understanding of the physical world.

Through this understanding, we can explore altered states of consciousness and gain insights into the mysteries of existence.

12. Holograms

Holograms represent a fascinating concept, wherein data is replicated in a three-dimensional form. The term "hologram" is derived from the Greek words "holos," meaning "whole," and "gramma," meaning "message," symbolizing the creation of a complete picture or message through duplication.

ORIGINAL CIA REPORT SUMMARY AND OVERVIEW:

Energy can produce, store, and retrieve meaning in the universe by virtue of the frequencies at which it projects or expands into three-dimensional space to create a living hologram. The concept of the hologram can be most easily understood by using an example cited by Bentov in which he asks the reader to visualize a bowl full of water into which three pebbles are dropped. As the ripples created by the simultaneous entry of the three pebbles radiate outward toward the rim of the bowl, Bentov further asks the reader to visualize that the surface of the water is suddenly flash frozen so that the ripple pattern is preserved instantly. The ice is removed leaving the three pebbles still laying at the bottom of the bowl. Then the ice is exposed to a powerful, coherent source of light, such as a laser. The result will be a three-dimensional model or representation of the position of the three pebbles suspended in midair.

The sheer amount of detail that can be encoded in a hologram is one of the many things that make it possible to magnify a holographic projection of a glass of swamp water and view tiny organisms not visible to the naked eye when looking at the glass itself. The concept of holography, despite its scientific implications, has only been known to physicists since the underlying mathematical principles were worked out by Dennis Gabor in 1947 (he later won a Nobel Prize for his work).

Laboratory demonstration of Gabor's work occurred years later following the invention of the laser. As biologist Lyall Watson explains:

"The purest kind of light available to us is that produced by a laser, which sends out a beam in which all the waves are of one frequency, like those made by an ideal pebble in a perfect pond. When two laser beams touch, they produce an interference pattern of light and dark ripples that can be recorded on a photographic plate. And if one of the beams, instead of coming directly from the laser, is reflected first off, an object such as a human face, the resulting pattern will be extraordinarily complex indeed, but it can still be recorded. The record will be a hologram of the face."

SUMMARY AND ADDITIONS:

Holograms present a complex concept, especially in their creation and reproduction. To capture multiple points of data, holograms rely on the interference of waves, which generates a 3D pattern. In comparison, conventional 2D images, like JPEGs, can distort and lose quality when resized. However, in vector images, each point contains detailed information, allowing for scaling without distortion.

Similarly, a hologram's interference pattern stores vast amounts of data from different waves or patterns, enabling more accurate duplication. This multiple-source information results in a more precise and realistic representation than a single 2D line could ever achieve. Understanding the nature of holograms enhances our appreciation for the intricate interplay of energy and the potential it holds for unlocking hidden aspects of the universe.

13. The Part Encodes the Whole

A remarkable property of holograms is their ability to encapsulate a complete dataset within the smallest part of the whole. Even if the hologram is divided into countless pieces, each fragment retains enough information to reconstruct the entire image individually.

ORIGINAL CIA REPORT SUMMARY AND OVERVIEW:

When a hologram is broken into millions of pieces, every single fragment retains the data necessary to recreate the entire holographic image, albeit with varying degrees of clarity and distortion. This extraordinary feature of holograms stems from the interaction of energy in motion with energy at rest or in a non-motion state. In the example of the pebbles and water, the pebbles represent energy in motion, while the still water symbolizes energy at rest. To perceive the hologram's meaning, coherent light, like a laser beam, is used to move energy through the interference pattern.

Dennis Gabor, the Nobel Prize laureate who laid the groundwork for holography, projected the three-dimensional holographic image into space while holding the interference pattern in front of the coherent light. The result is a highly efficient data storage system where billions of bits of information can be stored in a tiny space, and the pattern of the holographic photograph is distributed throughout the entire medium.

SUMMARY AND ADDITIONS:

The analogy of DNA serves well to understand the hologram's efficiency. Just as every strand of DNA contains the entire blueprint of an organism, a hologram contains the entire picture replicated in every minuscule portion of itself. This property of holograms opens the door to potential applications in data storage and information transmission, revealing the profound interconnectedness and complexity inherent in the universe's vibrational fabric.

14. The Consciousness Matrix

The theory proposed by Stanford University suggests that everything in the universe is interconnected as a hologram. In this context, our energetic consciousness plays a vital role in creating the holographic representation of ourselves. This holographic self-interacts with other energies and influences the creation of holograms representing our surroundings.

In essence, this theory implies that our consciousness and the surrounding energies form a dynamic interplay, constructing the intricate holographic web of reality. As we delve deeper into the Gateway Process, we explore the potential of this holographic interconnectedness and how it can be harnessed to expand our consciousness and access profound levels of understanding and knowledge.

ORIGINAL CIA REPORT SUMMARY AND OVERVIEW:

The universe is a vast interplay of interacting energy fields, some in motion and some at rest, forming an incredible holographic complexity. This holographic nature of the universe is not limited to the external world but also extends to the human mind, according to the theories put forth by Karl Pribram, a neuroscientist at Stanford University, and David Bohm, a physicist at the University of London.

In their understanding, the human mind acts as a hologram, attuning itself to the universal hologram through the exchange of energy. This process allows the mind to deduce meaning and attain consciousness. When we explore states of expanded or altered consciousness, as the Gateway Process does, this mechanism comes into play.

As energy traverses various aspects of the universal hologram, it is perceived by the electrostatic fields that form the human mind. The holographic images conveyed by this energy are projected upon these electrostatic fields and are understood or perceived to the extent that the fields operate at specific frequencies and amplitudes that can resonate with and "read" the energy carrier wave pattern.

Changes in the frequency and amplitude of the electrostatic field in the human mind influence the configuration and character of the holographic energy matrix projected by the mind. This matrix allows the mind to directly intercept and comprehend the meaning conveyed by the holographic transmissions of the universe.

To make sense of the holographic image received, the mind then compares it with its own internal hologram, which includes memory and past experiences. By registering differences in geometric form and energy frequency between the incoming holographic information and its own internal hologram, the consciousness perceives and interprets the incoming data. This process enables us to navigate and understand the intricacies of the holographic reality in which we exist.

(see Exhibit 2).

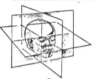

CONSCIOUSNESS ENERGY GRID

Left Hemisphere
Consciousness Grid

Acts like the Mind's
computer software to
reduce input from right
hemisphere to verbal
symbols and concepts.

Right Hemisphere
Consciousness Grid

Reduces three dimension
holographic image to tw
dimensional go/no go fo:

Exhibit 2: The functions of brain hemispheres in consciousness. Taken from the CIA Document.

As psychologist Keith Floyd puts it:

"Contrary to what everyone knows is so, it may not be the brain that produces consciousness — but rather, consciousness that creates the appearance of the brain…"

Clearer image for exhibit 2

Consciousness Energy Grid

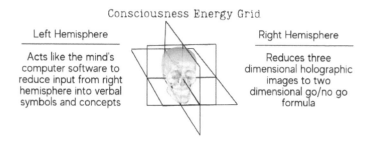

Left Hemisphere	Right Hemisphere
Acts like the mind's computer software to reduce input from right hemisphere into verbal symbols and concepts	Reduces three dimensional holographic images to two dimensional go/no go formula

SUMMARY AND ADDITIONS:

If we view everything as energetic holograms, our perception and interaction with the world take on a whole new dimension. The concept of the universe as a vast interplay of energy fields allows us to recognize that our consciousness is intricately entwined with these energies. As a result, we have the potential to influence and be influenced by the holographic reality in which we exist.

Using the understanding of energy and holographic principles, the Gateway Process offers a pathway to explore altered states of consciousness and different realities. By consciously working with our energetic fields and resonant frequencies, we can attune ourselves to specific holograms or spaces in time. Through imagination and intentional shifts in our resonant frequencies, we open the door to perceiving and interacting with different aspects of the holographic universe.

This concept aligns with the idea that consciousness creates reality, and by consciously engaging with the energetic holograms around us, we can alter our experience and understanding of the world. It implies that the boundaries we perceive in the physical realm might be more malleable than we initially thought. By harnessing the power of our consciousness and energy, we can potentially transcend the limitations of time and space, exploring different realms and accessing new dimensions of knowledge.

We are learning more about this today as we explore holography and AI learning models using energy signature and floor maps. Based on the pings of a wi-fi router or energy frequency of a room, scientists are training AI to know where people are in a room without any cameras with near perfect accuracy. It is this same concept that is used to understand energy frequency and holographic displacement.

The Gateway Process serves as a guide to assist individuals in navigating these energetic realms, providing tools and techniques to synchronize brain hemispheres, induce altered states of consciousness, and explore the vastness of the holographic universe. Through this journey, participants can expand their understanding of themselves and the interconnected nature of all things, realizing the boundless potential that lies within their own consciousness. In essence, the Gateway Process empowers individuals to become explorers of the energetic cosmos, traveling through the holographic tapestry of existence with intention and purpose.

15. Brain in Phase

The human brain can be likened to a remarkable supercomputer constantly processing and interpreting vast amounts of data from various sources. Our brains receive and analyze information from the world around us through our senses, and this input is then processed to form our understanding of reality. However, the brain's processing capabilities have certain limitations, and it often simplifies complex 3D information into more manageable 2D representations.

Just like a computer, the brain relies on established blueprints or patterns to interpret the data it receives. These blueprints are the result of our experiences, knowledge, and learned associations. When new information is encountered, the brain compares it to these existing patterns to make sense of it quickly and efficiently.

This process of pattern recognition and interpretation allows the brain to work rapidly, enabling us to navigate through our daily lives effectively. However, it can also lead to biases and cognitive shortcuts, as the brain may rely on preconceived notions rather than fully analyzing novel or unfamiliar information.

The Gateway Process acknowledges the brain's natural tendencies and seeks to expand its processing capabilities by introducing methods to synchronize brain hemispheres and access altered states of consciousness. By doing so, the Gateway Process aims to open the mind to new perspectives, knowledge, and experiences beyond the limitations of habitual thinking.

ORIGINAL CIA REPORT SUMMARY AND OVERVIEW:

The concept of the consciousness process becomes clearer when envisioning the holographic input overlaid with a three-dimensional grid system. This approach allows all energy patterns within to be defined through three-dimensional geometry. This complex data can then be mathematically streamlined into two dimensions. Bentov suggests that scientists propose the human mind operates on a basic binary system, a "go/no go" mechanism, much like digital computers.

With this understanding, when the mind overlays a three-dimensional matrix onto the holographic information it aims to interpret, and subsequently reduces this information to two dimensions through mathematical processes, it can effectively process it. This mirrors how man-made computers process data, making comparisons between stored information and incoming data. Our minds function similarly, perceiving through these comparative processes. Bentov succinctly phrases this concept:

"Our reality is shaped through ongoing comparisons... Our perception is always centered around differences."

In heightened states of consciousness, the right hemisphere of the brain, functioning holistically, non-linearly, and without words, acts as the primary receptor for this holographic input. Concurrently, the left hemisphere operates in phase with the right, serving as a secondary matrix. Its binary, computer-like operation screens and further reduces the data by means of comparison, ultimately transforming it into a distinct two-dimensional form.

SUMMARY AND ADDITIONS:

This dynamic interplay between the right and left hemispheres of the brain allows us to perceive and interpret the holographic nature of reality in a way that integrates both intuitive, holistic understanding and analytical, logical processing. The Gateway Process seeks to enhance and optimize this harmonious functioning of the brain's hemispheres, opening possibilities for expanded consciousness, access to higher states of being, and deeper insights into the nature of existence. By synchronizing and aligning the brain's hemispheres, individuals can explore and navigate the holographic universe with heightened clarity and coherence.

The concept of the holographic mind can be likened to interpreting an MRI readout. Just as an MRI captures slices of the human brain, our world is filled with vast amounts of data, some of which is visible to us, and some of which is not. This data exists on the surface, beneath the surface, and in the depths of reality. Some information is significant and relevant, while other aspects may not be as important.

When an MRI generates a 3D model of the brain, it gathers and interprets all the information obtained from the slices to create a comprehensive representation. Similarly, our holographic mind processes the energetic data it receives from the universe and forms a holistic understanding of our reality. It stores expectations and patterns based on this data, allowing us to navigate the world more efficiently. Just like a radiologist interpreting an MRI, our mind has learned to recognize familiar patterns and configurations in the holographic input.

When we encounter new information or stimuli, our holographic mind compares it to what is already known and familiar. It seeks out differences and discrepancies, just like the radiologist looks for anomalies or abnormalities in the MRI readout, such as a large tumor. Rather than constructing an entirely new hologram from scratch, our mind uses existing templates and modifies them based on the differences observed. This process allows us to perceive and understand the world around us more effectively, making sense of the data we encounter and integrating it into our existing knowledge and experiences.

In the context of the Gateway Process, the goal is to optimize this holographic processing of information, enhancing our ability to perceive subtle differences, access higher states of consciousness, and explore the interconnectedness of reality on a deeper level. By fine-tuning our holographic mind and harmonizing the functioning of our brain's hemispheres, we can unlock new potential and insights within ourselves and the universe we inhabit.

16. Evaluation

While we may not have a conventional name for this "sense" that allows us to receive and interpret energetic data, the perception of these energies is undoubtedly present in human experience. Throughout history, various cultures, mystics, and spiritual practitioners have attested to their ability to work with and harness these subtle energies for healing, spiritual growth, and intuitive insights.

ORIGINAL CIA REPORT SUMMARY AND OVERVIEW:

Gateway's success lies in its ability to refine the energy matrix of the mind.

This accomplishment leads to the expansion and alteration of human consciousness, enabling perception beyond the confines of physical senses. As a result, individuals become capable of perceiving more of the universal hologram, a realm inaccessible through ordinary sensory perception. Marilyn Ferguson observes that the ideas put forth by Pribram and Bohm seem to encompass all forms of transcendental experiences, paranormal occurrences, and even what might be considered "normal" perceptual anomalies.

Ferguson then highlights Pribram's revolutionary proposition:

Presently, he presents a groundbreaking, all-encompassing model that has stirred significant enthusiasm among those captivated by the enigma of human consciousness. His "holographic model" unites brain research with theoretical physics, providing an explanation for regular perception while simultaneously demystifying paranormal and transcendental experiences. It relegates them from the realm of the supernatural and aligns them with the laws of nature.

Similar to the peculiar revelations of quantum physics, this theory's profound shift in perspective suddenly brings clarity to the enigmatic teachings of mystics throughout history.

SUMMARY AND ADDITIONS:

Science and fiction have often been regarded as separate realms, with the latter representing imaginative and speculative storytelling. However, as McDonell completes his training in the Gateway Process, it seems he might have become convinced that some elements of fiction may not be entirely untrue. This realization fuels his desire to bridge the gap between the two, recognizing that human experiences and beliefs have explored outrageous destinations that science is now starting to unveil.

Throughout history, humans have claimed to communicate with energies, spirits, and distant beings. Mystics have asserted their ability to control elements and transcend their physical bodies. While these claims have often been dismissed as fiction or superstition, the Gateway Process opens the possibility that these abilities may not be entirely unfounded. By tapping into the energetic fabric of the universe, the Gateway Process suggests that previously unexplained abilities could become commonplace.

As scientific discoveries unfold, correlations emerge between mystical experiences and principles found in quantum physics, neuroscience, and other scientific disciplines. The concept of the universe as a holographic and interconnected whole, composed of interacting energy fields, aligns with ancient spiritual beliefs of interconnectedness and oneness.

The Gateway Process explores the confluence of science and spirituality, acknowledging that the human mind can access higher states of consciousness and information beyond conventional sensory perception. This aligns with the practices of mystics and spiritual seekers who have long delved into meditation, energy work, and altered states of consciousness to explore unseen realms and subtle energies.

By bridging the gap between science and spirituality, the Gateway Process reveals that these ancient practices and beliefs hold profound truths about the nature of reality. It provides a framework for understanding and harnessing these energies to achieve personal growth, expanded consciousness, and a deeper connection to the universe.

Through this exploration, we begin to appreciate the wisdom passed down by generations of spiritual practitioners and recognize the potential for integrating this understanding with modern scientific insights. The convergence of these perspectives opens up new possibilities for humanity to expand our consciousness and gain a profound understanding of ourselves, the world, and the interconnectedness that binds all things together.

17. Self-Cognition

Indeed, the unique gift of self-cognition sets humans apart from other living beings in our world. Our ability to reason, understand, and create objective standards allows us to navigate and shape the world in extraordinary ways. This cognitive prowess enables us to imagine possibilities beyond our immediate reality and to bring those visions into existence through our actions and creations.

Through the energetic field that surrounds us, we possess the capacity to transform not only ourselves but also the world around us. Our thoughts, emotions, and intentions emit energetic frequencies that can interact with the larger energetic fabric of the universe.

By harnessing and directing this energy, we have the potential to influence our experiences, manifest our desires, and impact the course of events.

ORIGINAL CIA REPORT SUMMARY AND OVERVIEW:

To provide a comprehensive overview of the process through which the mind attains and exercises consciousness, it is essential to elucidate the mechanism responsible for a distinct facet of human thought: self-cognition. Unlike the consciousness observed in plants or animals, humans possess not only awareness but also the unique capacity for metacognition.

In essence, human beings are not only conscious, but they are also conscious of their consciousness. They possess the ability to monitor and observe their own thought processes. Furthermore, they can engage in comparative analysis, evaluating the functioning of their thoughts against various predefined "objective" criteria. This unique attribute of human consciousness is rooted in its capability to replicate segments of its own hologram, project these replicas outward, "perceive" this projection, compare it with the memory component (housing its evaluative standards), and assess the disparities using a framework of three-dimensional geometry. This assessment is ultimately distilled into a binary "go/no go" signal that translates into verbal cognition.

SUMMARY AND ADDITIONS:

Throughout history, philosophers and mystics have contemplated the human ability to "Know thyself" with profound statements like "I am, therefore I am" and "I think, therefore I am." These discoveries reflect our awareness and cognition of our own existence. However, conventional understanding often portrays this as a one-way communication, where we perceive and receive understanding from external sources. Delving into the energetic truth of our existence reveals a more profound reality—a two-way communication process.

In this exploration of energetic consciousness, we not only receive and perceive but also have the power to project and send data or creative intentions into the energetic realm. By doing so, we imprint our desires on the collective, influencing and shaping the collective experience accordingly.

This profound creative power is not limited to the physical realm alone. It extends into the realm of consciousness, where we can explore higher states of being and connect with the deeper aspects of our existence. Through this connection, we gain access to vast reservoirs of wisdom, insight, and understanding that transcend ordinary sensory perception.

This energetic field serves as a conduit for our intentions, dreams, and aspirations. By aligning ourselves with the greater energetic whole and focusing our intentions, we can bring about meaningful transformations in our lives and the world around us. This co-creation with the energetic universe empowers us to explore the depths of our potential and unravel the mysteries of our existence.

As we explore further, we come to recognize that our consciousness is not confined to our physical bodies or the material world. It extends beyond the boundaries of time and space, enabling us to connect with the eternal and infinite aspects of existence. Embracing the nature of our energetic consciousness, we embark on a journey of self-discovery and self-realization, unlocking the full extent of our capabilities as conscious beings.

Ultimately, the benefit of being human lies in our capacity to engage with the profound mysteries of existence and to shape the world with the power of our thoughts, intentions, and creative abilities. Through the dynamic interplay with the energetic field, we become active co-creators of our reality, influencing the course of events and evolving our consciousness in the process. This transformative journey offers boundless opportunities to explore the depths of our potential and make a meaningful impact on the world and the lives of others.

18. Time-Space Dimension

Time and space are concepts that arise from the limitations and boundaries of our human perception. In a finite and changing world, we use these concepts to measure and define the passing of moments and the extension of objects in space. However, when we transcend these limitations and perceive existence from a higher perspective, the constructs of time and space lose their relevance.

Imagine a glass of water taken from the vast ocean. Within the confines of the glass, we can perceive a distinct entity separate from the ocean. Yet, when we remove the boundaries of the glass, the water merges seamlessly back into the ocean, becoming indistinguishable from the rest of the vast expanse.

ORIGINAL CIA REPORT SUMMARY AND OVERVIEW:

Our exploration of the Gateway process has thus far been straightforward, laying the foundation for a deeper understanding. Now, we enter the realm of true fascination. The Gateway process encompasses more than just the perception of aspects of the universal hologram accessible within the dimensions of time-space as we recognize it. Our task now is to unravel the mechanism by which human consciousness can transcend the boundaries of time-space. To achieve this, it's imperative to grasp the fundamental concepts of time and space, which will illuminate how these dimensions can be transcended.

In the realm of physics, time is characterized as a measure of energy or force in motion, essentially quantifying change. Yet, for energy to be in motion, it must be confined within certain vibrational patterns. This confinement grants it a specific location distinct from other locations, effectively defining what we understand as space. Energy not bound by such confines exists as an unbounded force, a limitless essence. This energy is beyond time, for it holds no boundaries or dimensions, transcending the limits of our understanding.

Similarly, this unconfined energy is beyond the confines of space as well. The concept of space implies the presence of specific energy forms in specific locations, distinguishing one "here" from another "there." However, when energy is infinite, such distinctions vanish, and the sense of area ceases to exist. This energy extends limitlessly, devoid of beginning, end, or location. It embodies conscious force, the elemental power of existence without form – a state of boundless being. While it remains conscious, it does not generate holograms while in this state of complete rest. Instead, it passively perceives the holograms generated by the energy in motion across the various dimensions of our created universe. However, it eludes the perception of consciousness engaged in the active universe.

This state of inactive infinity is termed by physicists as the "Absolute." Between the Absolute and the material universe, where we experience our physical reality, there exist intermediary dimensions accessible through altered states of consciousness. Theoretically, human consciousness can expand its perceptual horizons until it reaches the dimension of the Absolute. At this juncture, perception halts, as the Absolute generates no holograms about itself.

In this intricate interplay of energy, dimensions, and consciousness lies the gateway to a deeper understanding of our reality and existence.

SUMMARY AND ADDITIONS:

In essence, our perception gives rise to our physical existence. We exist because our human minds perceive boundaries—those of time and space. Our perception creates the matter that constitutes our reality. The "Absolute," lacking perception and holographic generation, exists beyond matter. If our consciousness were to expand to perceive the Absolute, it would cease to be.

As illustrated in our earlier example, when the glass of water returns to the ocean, it is no longer a separate entity. Though its molecules persist, the perception of it as a glass of water vanishes, and it becomes indistinguishable from the ocean.

Likewise, in the realm of existence, our individuality arises from the boundaries of time and space we perceive. Yet, when we expand our consciousness beyond these limitations, we discover our interconnectedness with all of existence. In this expanded state, the confines of the individual self dissolve, and we merge with the Absolute, encompassing everything.

In this profound unity, time and space lose their significance as we transcend their limitations. We become part of the eternal fabric of existence, where the concept of "I" becomes irrelevant, and we experience the vastness of the Absolute.

In this understanding, existence surpasses the confines of the individual self and embraces the infinite nature of reality. We are no longer bound by time and space but join the cosmic dance of existence, harmoniously integrated with the vast ocean of the Absolute.

The Gateway Process

90

19. Intervening Dimensions

To discuss dimensions, we must first understand what Planck's Length is. Max Planck, the originator of quantum theory, introduced this concept. It represents the smallest possible distance in the known universe, beyond which anything smaller would collapse into a black hole. This base unit is calculated using an equation involving three fundamental constants: the speed of light, the Planck constant, and the gravitational constant. The Planck Length is considered the theoretical minimum distance, akin to a zero point. It is a measurement so infinitesimally small that if visualized as a wave pattern, it would appear as a straight line.

ORIGINAL CIA REPORT SUMMARY AND OVERVIEW:

The Absolute, existing as conscious energy without confines, permeates every dimension, including our familiar time-space dimension of physical existence. Yet, while it envelops all, it remains imperceptible to us. This notion holds true for the intervening dimensions that various energies traverse, moving to and from their origin in the state of infinity – the Absolute.

For human consciousness to venture into these intermediary dimensions, an intense focus is required. This heightened focus prompts the frequency of the energy pattern constituting our consciousness (the brainwave output) to accelerate significantly. As this frequency pattern approaches a solid line on an oscilloscope, it inches closer to an altered state of consciousness. This phenomenon is rooted in Planck's Distance, a physics principle that dictates that any oscillating frequency will reach two points of complete rest, delineating each oscillation.

These points of rest are critical for oscillation patterns, allowing the energy to shift direction and sustain its vibrations within defined limits. Astonishingly, at the instant when energy briefly rests at one of these points, it momentarily "clicks out" of time-space and melds into infinity – an extraordinary occurrence depicted in Exhibit 3 (see image).

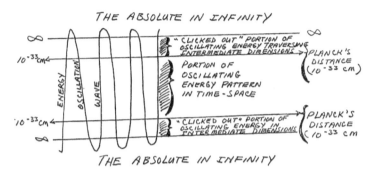

Exhibit 3: The display of the clicked-out phenomenon. Taken from the CIA Document.

The threshold to cross this boundary lies where oscillation speed falls below 1e-33 centimeters per second – Planck's Distance. In Bentov's words, this is where "quantum mechanics tells us that when distances fall below Planck's Distance… we enter, in effect, a new world."

Returning to our analogy, human consciousness exhibits such a rapid frequency that the "click outs" almost fuse into a continuous pattern. Within this pattern, a portion of consciousness is theorized to engage in information gathering within the dimensions bridging time-space and the Absolute. Thus, as this nearly uninterrupted "click out" pattern aligns itself in continuous phase at speeds below Planck's Distance, but before reaching complete rest, human consciousness embarks on a journey akin to Alice stepping into Wonderland.

The Gateway experience, coupled with the Hemi-Sync® technique, seems designed to empower human consciousness to establish a cohesive pattern of perception within dimensions governed by speeds below Planck's Distance. With systematic and patient practice, this holds true whether our consciousness remains within the physical body or ventures beyond in the out-of-body state. Through this lens, the Gateway experience opens doors to dimensions once hidden, enhancing our understanding of existence itself.

SUMMARY AND ADDITIONS:

To access the state of being where one can interact with Absolute energies or perceive other dimensions, it is essential to align the energy or brainwave oscillations to the smallest possible length, known as the Planck Length. In this state, the energy wave pattern has distinct crests and troughs. At each crest and trough, the energy enters the realm of the Absolute and then returns.

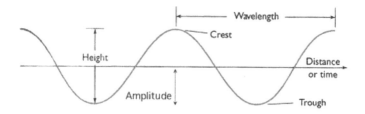

Imagine a square wave pattern where, each time it hits a crest or trough, it moves over one unit. If the wave has a high amplitude (i.e., height), it will take longer to travel compared to a wave with a low amplitude. It must travel from absolute crest to absolute trough, then over one unit, and again from absolute trough to absolute crest and over one unit for a complete oscillation. When the amplitude (the distance between crest and trough) is very low, approaching Planck

Length, the wave pattern essentially becomes a straight flat line, moving at an incredibly fast and nearly immeasurable speed. At every crest and trough, the energy enters the realm of the Absolute, and its presence becomes less focused in the physical world and primarily in the Absolute.

It is worth noting that the heart rate, which is influenced by the rate of human brainwave oscillations, shows as a straight flat line on an electrocardiogram (EKG) when there is no energetic presence (such as when a person passes away). When the energy is physically present in a material form, the rate of oscillation is slower compared to when the energy is without a physical form. This illustrates how the energetic state of consciousness influences the physical manifestation of life and the interconnectedness between energy, consciousness, and the physical realm.

20. Subatomic Particles

The phenomenon known as quantum entanglement involves subatomic particles becoming correlated in such a way that the state of one particle is directly connected to the state of another, regardless of the distance between them. This connection appears to be instantaneous, happening faster than the speed of light, and it is believed to happen outside of the boundaries of time and space as we understand them.

When two particles become entangled, they form a single quantum system, and any change in one particle's state will instantaneously affect the state of the other particle, no matter how far apart they are. This instantaneous connection between entangled particles challenges classical physics and has led to intriguing discussions and investigations about the nature of reality and the interconnectedness of the universe.

The concept of particles "clicking out" to communicate could be a way of visualizing this mysterious and non-local communication that occurs between entangled particles. Quantum entanglement is still an area of ongoing research and exploration, and it has profound implications for our understanding of the fundamental fabric of the universe.

ORIGINAL CIA REPORT SUMMARY AND OVERVIEW:

The behavior of subatomic particles presents a fascinating example of the "clicking out" phenomenon discussed earlier. In an article for Science Digest magazine, Dr. John Gliedman explores how subatomic particles communicate with each other after their energy fields become entrained due to colliding. This communication is believed to occur during the "click out phase" of the oscillation of the energy fields that make up these particles, enabling cross-communication at apparent speeds faster than light within the time-space dimension.

It's essential to note that this communication doesn't invalidate Einstein's Theory of Relativity; instead, it occurs outside of the confines of the time-space dimension governed by the Theory of Relativity. Dr. Gliedman explains:

"Quantum theory postulates a kind of long-range Siamese twin effect whenever two

subatomic particles collide and then go their separate ways. Even when the particles are halfway across the universe from each other, they instantaneously respond to each other's actions. And in so doing, they violate relativity's ban on faster-than-light velocities."

Indeed, regarding attempts to quantify what is known about the behavior of energy in dimensions apparently outside of time-space, Bentov speaks about,

"… courageous physicists who are working on hypothetical particles, called 'Tachyons,' which can move at speeds higher than light. The speed of tachyons starts just above the speed of light and ranges all the way to infinite velocities."

SUMMARY AND ADDITIONS:

Researchers have conducted studies that support the theory of non-local communication, where cells from a person are removed and taken to a distant location, yet they continue to react to changes happening with the original organism. Similarly, Energy Healers have demonstrated the ability to receive a person's cells, and later, if those cells are still viable, they can send energetic healing to the individual, which can be measured and observed in the person who provided the sample. Additionally, Energy Healers have been known to facilitate energetic healing without the use of genetic tissue.

Furthermore, a theory put forward by Dr Bruce Lipton, demonstrates how reincarnation is possible through similar processes to quantum entanglement, where your cells are like a receptor for your own specific incarnation, in very simplistic terms, almost as though your soul expression is dialed in to your cells like a TV antenna.

These findings and experiences align with the concept of non-local communication and energy transfer, seemingly transcending the limitations of time and space. Such phenomena challenge our traditional understanding of science and suggest that what was once considered fiction may indeed have tangible and scientifically observable aspects that are yet to be fully understood. As science continues to explore and expand its horizons, it may shed further light on these intriguing and transformative aspects of human consciousness and energy interaction.

21. Dimensions In-between

As humanity continues to explore the nature of existence and consciousness, we find ourselves with a strong grasp on our physical reality and the physical laws that govern it. However, as we venture into the realms beyond the known dimensions of time and space, we encounter questions and uncertainties about what lies in between.

When we slip in-between dimensions, the conventional laws of physics that we understand may not fully apply or may manifest differently. These uncharted territories challenge our traditional understanding of reality and open possibilities that go beyond our current scientific knowledge.

Exploring these in-between dimensions can be both exciting and daunting. While some aspects may align with our known physical laws, there could be phenomena that seem unfamiliar and potentially unpredictable. The laws of physics, as we currently comprehend them, might not provide a complete explanation for all the experiences and observations in these unexplored dimensions.

As we delve into the mysteries of these realms, we must approach them with an open mind and a willingness to expand our understanding. There may be other laws or principles at play that we have yet to discover or comprehend fully. While this can be a source of fear or uncertainty, it also presents an opportunity for growth, learning, and profound discoveries about the nature of reality.

It is essential for us to approach these explorations with caution and respect for the unknown. Just as we do in scientific research, we need to be observant, methodical, and willing to adjust our theories as we gain more insights. By embracing this journey with humility and curiosity, we can navigate the uncharted territories of consciousness and existence, leading us to a deeper understanding of ourselves and the vastness of the universe we inhabit.

ORIGINAL CIA REPORT SUMMARY AND OVERVIEW:

Now that we have considered the possibility that energy forms composing consciousness can extend beyond the time-space dimension, let's focus on the energy forms that exist in the dimensions between time-space and the Absolute. By doing so, we may gain a clearer understanding of the nature of "reality" in these intermediate realms.

According to Bentov, in these dimensions, the usual causal relationship between events breaks down, and movements may appear jerky rather than smooth. Both time and space can become "grainy" or "chunky." In this context, a particle of matter may traverse a piece of space without being synchronized with a specific moment in time, and events occur not causally but seemingly by random fluctuations.

In the time-space dimension, there is a proportional relationship between time and space, and their connection is predictable. Energy moving in particle or wave form can cover a certain space within a certain time with a specific velocity. However, in the intermediate dimensions, these constraints on energy oscillations are not uniform. As a result, we may encounter various distortions and inconsistencies that challenge our familiar assumptions about the relationship between time and space.

In these realms beyond time and space, access to both the past and the future becomes possible as the constraints of the current time-space dimension are abandoned. This opens new possibilities and challenges our conventional notions of causality and temporal linearity. By exploring these intermediate dimensions, we may gain profound insights into the nature of existence and consciousness beyond our usual perceptions.

SUMMARY AND ADDITIONS:

Dimensional travel is a theoretical concept that suggests we could potentially traverse the past or future by synchronizing our frequency with that of the Absolute and slipping into a dimension beyond our current perception. In this view, these dimensions would contain different aspects of time and reality, allowing us to access moments from our past or potential future.

However, the idea of dimensional travel raises questions about how we would distinguish our own past or future from other possible dimensions that might be foreign to us. If such dimensions exist, they could be just as real and physical as our current experience of reality.

It's important to note that the concept of dimensional travel moves into the realm of theory and speculation. While McDonnell underwent training related to these ideas, the experiences and theories surrounding dimensional travel are still in the exploratory and conceptual stages.

In this overview, we have touched on these concepts to provide insight into the profound questions and possibilities that arise when exploring the nature of consciousness and existence beyond our conventional understanding.

22. Special Status, OBE

With practice and persistent effort, individuals can learn to resonate at a higher level, enabling them to move their consciousness out of their physical bodies. In this out-of-body state, they may find it easier to traverse and interact with other dimensions.

Furthermore, once someone can project their consciousness out-of-body, their energy becomes more engaged with the higher realms. Similar to the behavior of subatomic particles, their energy leaves residue or becomes entrained, allowing them to vibrate at elevated levels more effortlessly. This heightened state of vibration facilitates better connection and understanding of messages from these higher dimensions.

ORIGINAL CIA REPORT SUMMARY AND OVERVIEW:

With enough practice, human consciousness can transcend the time-space dimension and connect with other energy systems in different dimensions. Achieving an out-of-body state is crucial for this process to be successful.

When a person becomes proficient in out-of-body movement and can break free from time-space while out of their body, they gain an advantage. Starting from a higher point in these dimensions allows the part of their consciousness involved in "clicking out" to have more time to interact with dimensions beyond time-space, as the intervening layers can be traversed more quickly.

Additionally, once the individual projects their consciousness beyond time-space, their consciousness naturally adjusts its frequency to the new energy environment, enhancing the focus and oscillating pattern. This self-reinforcing process promotes even further travel into these dimensions.

The preliminary conclusion is that the out-of-body state proves to be an effective way of accelerating the expansion of consciousness and interacting with dimensions beyond time and space. For Gateway technique practitioners, focusing efforts on achieving and utilizing the out-of-body state may yield faster and more remarkable results compared to expanding consciousness solely from a physical standpoint.

SUMMARY AND ADDITIONS:

Indeed, the exploration of consciousness and its potential to transcend the limitations of time and space is a central focus for those interested in metaphysics and mystical experiences. This higher state of consciousness is often associated with the frequency that psychics, mediums, and mystics tap into when they communicate messages from other realms.

While a deep understanding of the scientific aspects is not necessary to connect with these messages, comprehending the underlying science can undoubtedly enhance the depth and breadth of our connections. The knowledge of how consciousness interacts with energy fields and dimensions allows for a more profound appreciation of the interconnectedness of all things.

Whether approached from a scientific or spiritual perspective, the journey of exploring consciousness and connecting with higher realms offers profound insights and transformative experiences. It opens doors to new possibilities and expands our understanding of existence and the nature of reality. Ultimately, the exploration of consciousness leads to a richer and more meaningful experience of life, empowering us to connect with the mysteries of the universe in extraordinary ways.

23. Absolute in Perspective

McDonnell pauses at this point to summarize his exploration highlighting how so far it has delved into the fascinating interplay between consciousness, energy fields, and dimensions. He introduces the concept of the Absolute, a state of conscious energy beyond time and space, and discusses how human consciousness can potentially transcend the limitations of our physical reality.

ORIGINAL CIA REPORT SUMMARY AND OVERVIEW:

At this juncture, it is beneficial to reflect on the key aspects of our intellectual journey, encompassing the transition from time-space to the realm of the Absolute. We have delved into the intricacies of the hologram, a complex interplay of energy patterns from all dimensions of the universe, including time-space.

Our exploration has illuminated the profound nature of the human mind, comprised of energy fields that interact with the hologram, allowing us to deduce meaningful information. Through the left hemisphere of our brains, this data is processed into a usable form for our cognitive process, commonly known as thinking.

The hologram, in essence, represents the finite manifestation of the infinite consciousness of the Absolute, existing as active, energy-based form. The Absolute stands as the boundless wellspring of energy in perfect rest, forming the foundation from which the physical universe emerges and derives its existence.

In analogy, Bentov likens the dimension of the Absolute to the serene depths of a vast sea, while the turbulent waves above represent the familiar physical universe. The currents in between symbolize energy transitioning between states of rest and activity, either approaching infinity or departing from it.

As we continue our journey of exploration and understanding, the intricate interconnectedness of consciousness, energy, and dimensions continues to unfold, offering us deeper insights into the mysteries of existence.

24. From Big Bang to Torus

Bentov's model of the universe, from creation to continuation, parallels the widely accepted understanding of the human energy field. According to this model, energy radiates from the heart, moving in an upward direction. Upon reaching the crown chakra at the top of the head, it then expands in all directions, eventually descending back down to gather in the root chakra, thus initiating the cycle once more. Throughout the universe, we observe repeating patterns and designs that manifest in various forms, from the microscopic to the macroscopic level.

ORIGINAL CIA REPORT SUMMARY AND OVERVIEW:

Bentov's conceptual model illustrates the process of time-space evolution and the positioning of the universal hologram, drawing from the widely accepted "Big Bang" theory. This hologram, often referred to as a "Torus," is envisioned as a massive, self-contained spiral. Based on recent studies on the distribution of quasars (quasi-stellar objects) and the principle that smaller processes mirror larger ones in the universe, Bentov proposes the following scenario.

He draws parallels from the observed ability of quasars to emit highly concentrated beams of matter from their interiors, resembling a controlled, nonconcentric version of the "Big Bang." He envisions a similar process occurring during the universe's formation (see Exhibit 4).

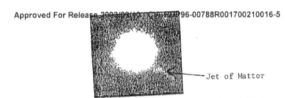

Figure A Photograph of Quaser Emitting Jet of Matter

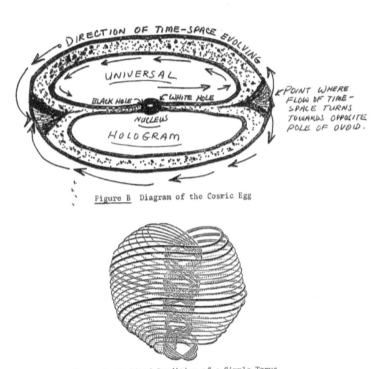

Figure B Diagram of the Cosmic Egg

Figure C Stylized Rendition of a Simple Torus

Exhibit 4: Figures A and B from Bentov "Stalking the Wild Pendulum," Figure C from Purce "The Mystical Spirit." Taken from the CIA Document.

Bentov's model suggests that galaxies located to the north of our own galaxy are moving away faster than those to the south, and those to the east and west are farther apart. He interprets this as evidence that the initial jet of matter that expanded into our universe has curved back on itself, forming an ovoid or egg-shaped pattern. According to his concept, matter in our universe is expelled from an extremely compressed energy nucleus through a "white hole" and then re-enters the ovoid pattern, eventually exiting through a "black hole" at the far end.

In this model, time is viewed as a measure of the changes that occur as energy evolves into more complex forms while progressing along the distance from the white hole side of the nucleus, around the shell of this "cosmic egg," and into the black hole. Time begins as a measure of the evolutionary movement of energy, expelled from infinity and confined within limits by the consciousness of the Absolute, as it takes the journey around the shell of the egg towards the black hole at the far end.

Included is an updated rendition of Exhibit 4 for clarity.

<u>Figure A</u> Photograph of a quasar emitting a jet of matter

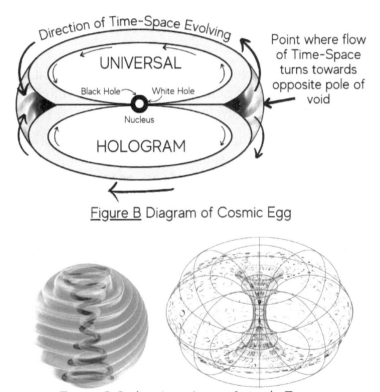

<u>Figure B</u> Diagram of Cosmic Egg

<u>Figure C</u> Stylized rendition of simple Torus

SUMMARY AND ADDITIONS:

In this proposed understanding, the human energy field follows a twisting and swirling pattern, like a gentle tornado. This energy pattern is concentrated and rotates through the chakras, with the heart chakra as the focal point where the twister meets the ground. The energy widens at the top before being released to fall. Although we don't observe debris being picked up and pulled back in, the entire pattern forms a swirling motion, tighter in the center as it rises and gradually becomes looser as it exits and falls. Once the energy falls to the bottom, it is then sucked back in and returns to cycle through again.

Using the as above so below understanding, it is postulated that like a human energy field, the universe has a similar energy cycle.

While understanding how the human energy field works can be beneficial for working with it, it is not a requirement to comprehend and engage with The Gateway Process. The Gateway Process provides a framework for exploring consciousness and its potential beyond time and space, irrespective of detailed knowledge about the intricacies of human energy patterns.

25. Our Place in Time

The Absolute encompasses the entire cosmic egg, as it is interconnected with everything. It exists as both the white hole that initiated the beginning of the universe and the black hole that draws everything back in. However, as human beings, we perceive ourselves with boundaries, and thus, we see our place within the unfolding of time and space in the spiral pattern. Our limited perspective allows us to experience the journey through time-space as we move along the spiral's trajectory.

ORIGINAL CIA REPORT SUMMARY AND OVERVIEW:

The observed distribution of galaxies leads us to believe that our universe is positioned near the top of the cosmic egg, where matter starts to curve back on itself. This explains why galaxies to the north appear to be moving away faster, as they are caught in the downward stream of matter heading toward the far end of the cosmic egg. This model helps us understand the dynamics of how matter is distributed and how galaxies are moving in relation to each other within the vast cosmic structure. (see Exhibit 5).

Exhibit 5: Relative Position of Our Galaxy in the Universe, From Bentov "Stalking the Wild Pendulum." Taken from the CIA Document.

The Absolute, which sustains the nucleus from which the original jet of matter emerged, exists layered over the cosmic egg. As the stream of matter moves around the ovoid towards the black hole, it generates an interference pattern within the cosmic egg, forming the universal hologram or Torus. This hologram encompasses the evolution of the universe in the past, present, and future, as it is

120

created simultaneously by matter in all phases of time.

Contemplating this model reveals how an altered and focused human consciousness could access information about the past, present, and future, as they coexist within the universal hologram. The future can be predicted or "seen" with total accuracy, given that all the consequences of the past and present converge in the hologram.

The interplay of energy patterns creates a complex four-dimensional hologram in a spiral shape, reflecting the multidimensional evolving pattern of the universe's evolution. The movements of the energies that constitute the universe leave their marks and tell their story over time, resulting in this intricate and ever-changing cosmic representation.

A clearer version of exhibit 5

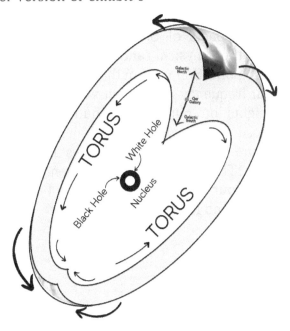

SUMMARY AND ADDITIONS:

In Bentov's depiction, our galaxy's position aligns with where the mind would be in a human energy field. This observation raises an intriguing question: Is our profound interest in understanding ourselves driven by our energetic connection to seeking knowledge and self-awareness?

Our human energy field, being part of the Absolute, lacks boundaries despite our attempts to define and confine it. It exists beyond the constraints of time and space, making it beyond our full perception. While we may sense energy, it is not experienced as tangible matter like our physical bodies or the world around us. Our current view and understanding are limited while we are bound to our physical energy.

The concept of using plant medicine like psilocybin and dimethyltryptamine (DMT) to explore the energetic aspects of ourselves and bridge the gap between the physical and energetic realms is a fascinating one. Some claim that these substances can raise our frequency to connect with the Absolute and gain insights into our energetic nature. The possibility that these plants were placed here to aid us in understanding our energetic selves is an intriguing question. The quest to comprehend the deeper aspects of our existence continues to be a subject of exploration and fascination.

26. Quality of Consciousness

The level of consciousness required to maintain a life form's hologram of reality is directly related to the complexity of that life form. The more intricate and sophisticated the life form, the greater the consciousness needed to sustain its perception of reality. In this sense, consciousness can be seen as infinite, just like the Absolute, without a definitive beginning or end.

On the other hand, reality, as experienced by a specific life form, is finite. It is shaped and perceived through the lens of that consciousness. When consciousness is no longer needed to uphold the hologram of reality associated with a life form, it returns to the infinite consciousness of the Absolute. This cycle continues, with consciousness transitioning between finite realities and the boundless Absolute, creating a dynamic interplay between the individual and the universal.

ORIGINAL CIA REPORT SUMMARY AND OVERVIEW:

As previously explained, the out-of-body state allows a significant portion of human consciousness to project beyond the physical body, enabling it to explore the terrestrial realm for information or venture into other dimensions beyond time-space to potentially interact with other forms of consciousness in the universe.

Consciousness serves as the organizing and sustaining force, directing energy within specific parameters to create a particular reality. When consciousness reaches a level of sophistication where it can perceive itself as its own hologram, it achieves self-cognition. Human beings possess this elevated form of consciousness, as does the Absolute. However, for the Absolute, self-cognition is a function of energy and its associated quality of consciousness in infinity, encompassing omniscience and omnipotence in a unified perception.

When energy returns to a state of complete rest within the Absolute, it reunites with the continuous pool of limitless and timeless perception residing there. Thus, the complexity of an energy system in its material or physical state determines the level of consciousness required to maintain its reality. Our individual consciousness is a distinct aspect of the universal consciousness within the Absolute. While the Absolute is responsible for organizing the energy patterns that compose our physical bodies, it remains separate and superior to them.

Consciousness exists beyond the boundaries of reality, transcending time and space, and therefore possesses no beginning or end. On the other hand, reality is confined by time and space, and thus has both a beginning and an end. Nevertheless, the fundamental quantum of energy and its associated consciousness is eternal. When a reality comes to an end, the essential energy simply returns to infinity within the Absolute.

SUMMARY AND ADDITIONS:

Indeed, the concept of consciousness can vary in quality and complexity among different life forms. While plants possess a form of consciousness, it is of a lower quality compared to human consciousness. There is no concrete evidence to suggest that plants are aware of themselves or possess self-cognition. Although there are new studies that are leaning toward uncovering this possibility. This is in part because they do exhibit intelligence, interconnectedness, and the ability to respond to their environment, indicating a level of consciousness. Additionally, for those that are able to see energy fields, they say that the energy of plants are some of the easiest to visualize.

Humans, on the other hand, possess a higher quality of consciousness that allows for self-awareness, complex emotions, and the ability to create and manifest new realities through thoughts, aspirations, and actions. This higher level of consciousness is necessary to animate and maintain the complex reality of a human body and mind.

When a physical body dies, the consciousness or soul, as some call it, leaves and returns to the Absolute, which is often referred to as God or the source of all existence. The physical form may remain, but the unique individual consciousness that animated and gave life to that form is no longer present. Every aspect of their hologram, including their thoughts, perceptions, and ability to impact the world, ceases to exist in its previous form. Instead, memories and stories shared by others become the way the person lives on in the minds of those who knew them.

In this way, consciousness is both unique and ephemeral, shaping and experiencing reality during its time in the physical form and eventually returning to the timeless pool of consciousness within the Absolute.

27. Consciousness in Perspective

Upon returning to the Absolute, each conscious being retains its memories and experiences as a distinct entity. These experiences become part of the collective consciousness within the Absolute, contributing to the larger whole of existence. So, while individual consciousness dissolves into the vast consciousness of the Absolute, the unique "story" of each being is preserved within the fabric of the collective.

As part of the Absolute, we maintain the ability to perceive and understand the entirety of existence, encompassing all that is and ever was. However, individual consciousness no longer possesses the capacity to create new holograms or make decisions as it did during its time in the physical form. Instead, it merges with the infinite pool of consciousness, becoming one with the boundless and eternal nature of the Absolute.

In this way, individual consciousness finds both unity and continuity within the larger framework of the Absolute, contributing its experiences and understanding to the tapestry of existence. While no longer operating as an independent entity, it remains an integral part of the timeless and limitless consciousness that underlies all of reality.

ORIGINAL CIA REPORT SUMMARY AND OVERVIEW:

When human consciousness dissociates from physical reality and interacts with other intelligences in different dimensions, it embarks on a journey that leads to the ultimate return to the Absolute. During this journey, consciousness accumulates memories that are as eternal as consciousness itself. As consciousness returns to the Absolute, it brings with it all the memories acquired through its experiences in reality.

However, the return to the Absolute does not mean the extinction of the individual identity that was sustained by consciousness during its journey. Instead, it leads to a merging of differentiated consciousness with the universal consciousness and infinity of the Absolute. The memories confer a separate identity and *self-knowledge to this consciousness, which remains intact even as it becomes part of the all-knowing infinite continuum of consciousness.*

Although this consciousness retains the ability to perceive, it loses the capacity for independent thought and decision-making, which is a characteristic of energy in motion. Nonetheless, this exchange grants it access to a higher level of understanding and unity with the boundless consciousness of the Absolute.

In the out-of-body state, a person projects this eternal spark of consciousness and memory, which constitutes the core of their identity, allowing it to explore and learn from dimensions beyond the time-space world where their physical form experiences its reality. This journey of consciousness offers profound insights and experiences, leading to a deeper connection with the infinite aspects of existence.

SUMMARY AND ADDITIONS:

Exactly, the analogy of the glass of ocean water beautifully illustrates the concept of merging and retaining memories in the context of consciousness and its journey back to the Absolute. When the water from the glass is returned to the ocean, it becomes one with the vast ocean, no longer separate. Yet, the water retains the memory of its experience of being in the glass, perceiving reality from that unique perspective, and existing within the confines of the glass.

Similarly, when consciousness returns to the Absolute, it becomes part of the larger whole, merging with universal consciousness. It retains the memories and experiences gathered throughout its journey in reality. Just like the water remembers its time in the glass, consciousness carries with it the knowledge and understanding it gained while existing in the physical form.

However, once merged with the Absolute, the individual consciousness can no longer be separated or re-created in its original form. It becomes an integral part of the infinite consciousness of the Absolute, with no individual identity or independent experiences. Just as the water can't be sorted back into its exact form after being mixed with the ocean, consciousness loses its ability to exist independently and is part of the vast continuum of the Absolute.

You might be familiar with the concept of the Akashic records, often associated with Edgar Cayce, the Sleeping Prophet. This explanation of returning to the Absolute created a connection for me as an explanation for how the records are created. As the Absolute, as it is explained in this report, it is without limits of time or space, when a consciousness returns to the absolute, its story, life, or information would return with it. In this way, no matter when or where that consciousness experienced itself in relation to our human perception, it would always be part of the record and accessible in any time or space.

28. Gateway Method

The Gateway process is conducted by continuously listening to the Hemi-Sync® Audios over time while following the instructions provided in the audios. To ensure proper brainwave synchronization, it is recommended to use headphones during the listening sessions, allowing each intended sound to reach the appropriate ear and corresponding hemisphere of the brain.

The duration of the training varies for each participant, as it depends on individual levels of self-development and experience in achieving a meditative or focused state of mind. Some participants may progress more quickly, while others may require more time to fully immerse themselves in the process and achieve the desired states of consciousness. Patience and consistent practice are key elements for success in the Gateway process.

ORIGINAL CIA REPORT SUMMARY AND OVERVIEW:

As discussed earlier, The Gateway Experience has been summarized by outlining its underlying structure, mechanisms, and intended purposes. Now, let's delve into the specific techniques that constitute the Gateway training process. These techniques are designed to empower users of the Hemi-Sync® audios to navigate the realms of high energy states, achievable through consistent engagement with the audios over an extended duration.

The time required to reach advanced energy states and master these techniques varies among individuals. Factors such as the sensitivity of one's nervous system, overall mental state, and prior experience in related practices like transcendental meditation play a role in determining the pace of progress.

The Gateway process commences by guiding participants to isolate distracting thoughts using an imagery tool called the "energy conversion box." Subsequently, participants learn a technique to synchronize their mind and body to attain a state of resonance. This involves repetitive chanting of a single tone, creating a prolonged and monotonous humming sound that triggers a sensation of vibration, especially in the head. By joining in this "resonant tuning," participants align their humming with a chorus of similar sounds on the Gateway tape.

132

Next, participants encounter the Gateway Affirmation, which they are encouraged to audibly repeat as it plays on the tape. This affirmation emphasizes that individuals are more than their physical bodies and expresses their deep desire for consciousness expansion.

SUMMARY AND ADDITIONS:

Hemi-Sync® is short for Hemispheric Synchronization, a brainwave synchronization technique developed by Robert Monroe, the founder of the Monroe Institute. It involves synchronizing the two hemispheres of the brain to create a Frequency Following Response (FFR), which is designed to induce specific effects. Monroe holds three patents on this technology.

The concept of binaural beats, a crucial element of Hemi-Sync®, was discovered in 1839 by H. W. Dove, a German experimenter. When an individual receives signals of two different frequencies, one to each ear, the brain detects a phase difference between these signals. If these signals are provided through speakers or stereo earphones, the brain interprets this phase difference as an anomaly, resulting in a binaural beat in an amplitude-modulated standing wave within each sound processing center of the brain. This effect can only be achieved when two singular sounds, one in each ear, are introduced simultaneously, with equal amplitude but different frequencies. The ideal frequency range for this phenomenon is typically between 4-8 hertz, and each frequency variation stimulates a different area of the brain.

The Hemi-Sync® method is designed to be experienced and practiced with headphones until the individual can recognize the corresponding feelings within their body associated with the different frequencies. The ultimate goal is for the person to be able to recreate these states of consciousness on their own, without the need for the Hemi-Sync® audios. With regular practice and familiarity, individuals can learn to access altered states of consciousness and enhance their personal growth and self-awareness through this technique.

Now is an opportune moment to shed light on a potential concern related to the current availability of Gateway audios. An independent researcher, who operates under the banner of the "Museum of Tarot," has conducted a study that is worth mentioning. This researcher maintains a presence on multiple social media platforms and purports to be a Neuroscientist. Additionally, he has recreated certain mind training devices based on his own research and studies.

While I tried to verify this information and identify the name of the influencer for this book, I encountered some limitations in doing so. Nonetheless, it is important to acknowledge this work as a potential avenue for your own exploration and investigation.

According to this researcher, he asserts and provides evidence that the current audios available may differ from the original ones. The implications of this variance are concerning even if they are not verified, as he also draws a connection between Robert

Monroe and the scientists responsible for developing the MK Ultra Program. It's worth considering these points and conducting your own research to form an informed perspective.

29. Hemi-Sync® Introduced

The participant is introduced to the audios with the understanding that they help synchronize the left and right brain. They are encouraged to create mental images or holograms to protect themselves in case they achieve out-of-body activity during the first session. In fact, for every subsequent session, they are asked to visualize this protective bubble.

ORIGINAL CIA REPORT SUMMARY AND OVERVIEW:

The participant is introduced to the Hemi-Sync® sound frequencies and encouraged to focus on and appreciate the feelings that accompany the synchronization of brainwaves. The next step involves progressive and systematic physical relaxation while listening to additional forms of "pink and white" noise. This aims to bring the physical body to the virtual threshold of sleep while calming the left hemisphere of the mind and heightening the attentiveness of the right hemisphere.

Once this state is achieved, the participant is guided to envision creating an "energy balloon" that flows from the center of the head down to the feet and back up again in all directions. This pattern resembles the cosmic egg discussed earlier and enhances bodily energy flow while facilitating a suitable resonant state. Additionally, the energy balloon is designed to provide protection against encountering lower energy-level entities if the participant achieves an out-of-body state, serving as a precautionary measure in the unlikely event of projecting outside the terrestrial sphere during the first out-of-body experience.

SUMMARY AND ADDITIONS:

Certainly, it is important to take precautions when exploring experiences involving foreign energies. While we cannot fully know what the Absolute contains, there is no need to fear the journey. We are already interconnected with the Absolute, and any energy we encounter is already a part of us.

Patience is key in this process. It should not be rushed, as it takes time to understand and navigate these experiences. Embrace the journey with an open mind and allow it to unfold naturally.

30. Advanced Techniques

As the participant starts to interact with the energy, they begin at Focus 10. The eight different techniques available for experience and interaction are problem-solving, patterning, color breathing, energy bar tool, remote viewing, live body mapping, travel into the past, and the future. However, it's important to note that not all of these focus levels are easily attainable. Many of them may require several months or even years of consistent practice to achieve. In the second part of this book, we will delve into each of these focus areas and explore the summary of the audios themselves.

ORIGINAL CIA REPORT SUMMARY AND OVERVIEW:

With the completion of Focus 10, the participant is now prepared to try to achieve a state of sufficiently expanded awareness that will allow him to engage in actual interaction with dimensions other than those associated with his experience of physical reality.

Starting at Focus 12 the participant is required to exert conscious effort while additional forms of "pink and white noise" are introduced into the sound stream that is being directed into his ears by the Gateway audio. Having attained this state of greatly expanded awareness, the participant is ready to begin employing a series of specific techniques or "tools," as the Monroe Institute refers to them, that enable him to manipulate his newly discovered expanded awareness to obtain practical, useful feedback that is valuable for promoting self-discovery and personal growth. The specific techniques that were used are described in greater detail below.

A. Problem Solving:

This technique involves identifying fundamental issues that the individual wishes to see resolved, filling his expanded awareness with his perception of these issues, and then projecting them out into the universe. In this way, the individual enlists the help of what Monroe Institute refers to as his "higher self," or expanded consciousness, to interact with the universal hologram to obtain the information needed to solve the problem.

This approach can be used to solve technical problems in physics, mathematics, and other sciences, as well as practical administrative problems, among other things, in addition to personal difficulties. Responses to the problem-solving technique can be received almost immediately, but most of the time they are based on developing intuition over the course of two to three days. Many times, the response manifests as a sudden, holistic perception in which the individual discovers that he simply knows the answer in all its ramifications and context, sometimes without being able to articulate his newly discovered perception, at least in the early stages. Sometimes the response will take the form of visual symbols, which the individual will be able to perceive with their minds while in the Focus 12 state and must decipher when they return to normal consciousness.

B. Patterning:

This process entails using one's consciousness to achieve desired outcomes in one's physical, emotional, or intellectual life. Concentration on the desired objective while in a Focus 12 state, extension of the individual's perception of that objective into the entire expanded consciousness, and projection of that perception into the universe with the intention that the desired objective is already a matter of existing achievement and is destined to be realized within the time frame specified are all components of this rite of passage.

143

The foundation for this methodology is the belief that the thought patterns generated by our consciousness when we are in a state of expanded awareness create holograms that represent the situation we want to create, laying the groundwork for actual realization of that goal. Once the desired objective's thought-generated hologram is established in the universe, it becomes a reality that interacts with the universal hologram to bring about the desired objective, which would not be possible under normal circumstances.

To put it another way, the patterning technique acknowledges that, because consciousness is the source of all reality, our thoughts have the ability to influence the development of reality in time-space as it applies to us if projected with sufficient intensity. The longer the universal hologram takes to reorient our reality sphere to accommodate our wishes, the more complicated the goal sought and the more radically it differs from our current reality. Monroe trainers advise against hastening the process because the individual may succeed in distancing himself from his current reality, which could be disastrous.

C. Color Breathing:

Color breathing is a technique that uses the expanded awareness and highly focused attentiveness associated with the Focus 12 state to imagine an assortment of colors in a particularly intense and vivid manner to use them to resonate with and activate the body's own energies. Fundamentally, it is a healing technique that aims to restore and improve the body's physical capabilities by

*balancing, revitalizing, and retuning
bodily energy flows.*

*It is based on the idea that the
electromagnetic field of the body can
change its resonance pattern to entrain
energy from the earth's electrostatic field
for its own use. The assorted colors
depicted in the technique remind the mind
as to which frequencies and amplitudes are
desired for this entrainment and the
resulting changes in bodily energy flow
patterns. Color's ability to influence the
human mind is well documented, as is its
efficacy in certain types of healing.*

*Applying intense blue light to an area of
inflammation in the body, for example,
results in a relatively quick and easily
observable reduction in swelling, whereas
red and, to a lesser extent, yellow have
the opposite effect. However, no external
light sources are used in the Hemi-Sync®
application of the technique, and the mind
is the sole agent of healing and
revitalization.*

D. Energy Bar Tool:

*Many cultures have folklore and occult
practices that include magic wands and
enchanted scepters. The scepters, staffs,
and maces carried by monarchs and high
priests alike appear with such frequency in
history that it suggests these items are at
the very least aspects of some type of
archetypical symbol that the human mind
seems to appreciate, perhaps quite
subliminally. In any case, the energy bar
tool technique entails imagining a small,
intensely pulsing dot of light that the
participant charges in his imagination with
enormous energy until it is almost pulsing.*

The participant then extrudes the dot into
the form of a sparkling, vibrating cylinder
of energy, which he uses to channel force
from the universe to specific parts of his
body for healing and revitalization.

E. Remote Viewing:

Furthermore, the energy bar tool is used as
a portal to initiate a follow-up technique
known as "remote viewing." In this context,
the participant transforms his energy bar
into a whirling vortex through which he
channels his imagination in search of new
and illuminating insights. The obvious
purpose of the symbolism involved in the
vortex appears to be to cue the
subconscious and convey instructions to it
in terms of nonverbal symbols that the
right hemisphere of the mind is capable of
understanding.

F. Living Body Map:

This technique amplifies the use of the
energy bar tool as a means of healing
specific areas or systems of the human
body. The participant's body is imagined,
and then the various major systems, such as
the nervous and circulatory systems, are
imagined in appropriate colors within the
confines of the imagined outline.

The energy bar tool is then used to
energize, balance, and heal the participant
in whatever way they desire. During the
procedure, the participant visualizes
various streams of colored energy flowing
out of the tool and into the organ system
or area being revitalized or healed.
Because colors are the result of different
wavelengths of light, or energy at

146

different frequencies, this technique is based on the assumption that because the human body is made up of energy, it can be vitalized and healed through the additive application of additional energy, provided that the energy is applied in the appropriate form.

G. Focus 15: Travel into the Past:

All of the preceding techniques are performed at the Focus 12 level of expanded awareness. The technique of time travel into the past, on the other hand, entails further expansion of consciousness via the inclusion of additional levels of sound on the Hemi-Sync® audios. Some of the sound is most likely just an intensification of the basic Hemi-Sync® frequencies, with the intention of further modifying brainwave frequency and amplitude.

Other aspects of the added sound patterns appear to be designed to provide subtle, almost subliminal suggestions to the mind as to what is desired via further expanded consciousness, in addition to the verbal suggestions and instructions also contained on the tape. Even the instructions are highly symbolic, with time portrayed as a massive wheel in the universe with various spokes, each of which provides access to a different part of the participant's past.

Focus 15 is an extremely advanced state that is extremely difficult to attain. During the approximately seven days of training, less than 5 percent of all participants in any given Gateway Experience fully achieve the Focus 15 state. Nonetheless, Monroe Institute trainers believe that with enough practice, Focus 15 can be attained. They also state that a person who has attained Focus 15 can examine not only the individual's history but also other aspects of the past with which the individual has no connection.

H. Focus 21: The Future:

The final and most advanced Focus state associated with the Gateway training program involves movement outside of time-space boundaries, as in Focus 15, but with an emphasis on discovering the future rather than the past.

The person who has attained this state has attained a truly advanced level. Except in unusual circumstances, it is most likely only attainable by those who have conditioned themselves through long periods of meditation or who have practiced long and hard using the Hemi-Sync® audios for months, if not years.

SUMMARY AND ADDITIONS:

During the week-long journey at the Monroe Institute, participants aim to reach various levels or procedures. The training focuses on skills and audio listening; it's not expected that participants will master all practiced skills.

It's important to note that, at the time of writing, the institute continues to offer these training sessions for those interested in attending.

This advanced training aligns with mystic circles' concepts known as clair abilities, which we can bridge here. While many Psychics, Mediums, and Mystics have been using these skills for generations, they haven't used a training method like this to access the skills. Many have either been born with gifts, have an event that creates the connections, or have the ability in their genetic bloodline.

"Clair" means "clear" and is coupled with a sense associated with it broadly referred to as Clair-Abilities. Below is a brief overview of these abilities:

CLAIRCOGNIZANCE – INTUITIVE KNOWLEDGE

Claircognizance is when a person possesses psychic knowledge without any apparent physical explanation. This ability includes precognition (knowledge of the future) and retrocognition (knowledge of the past). It also includes simple knowing, like the definition of words you have never heard, or the answer to a question you have no knowledge of.

CLAIRVOYANCE – INTUITIVE VISION

Clairvoyance allows individuals to see objects, actions, or events without using their physical eyes. This ability transcends time and space and might involve insights seen through the third eye (also known as the mind's eye).

CLAIRAUDIENCE – INTUITIVE AUDIO or HEARING

Clairaudience is the ability to perceive sounds, words, or extrasensory noises. These tones exist beyond conventional human experience, transcending space and time. Examples include sounds produced by the body, living things, nature, man-made objects, and their interactions, as well as ethereal sounds like voices of the deceased or mystical music.

CLAIRSENTIENCE – INTUITIVE KNOWING BY FEELING

Clairsentience refers to acquiring knowledge through feelings. A clairsentient person senses vibrations from others, animals, and places. This ability ranges from perceiving others' thoughts, emotions, illnesses, and injuries through feelings in the body. Unlike clairvoyance, this knowledge stems solely from bodily sensations.

CLAIRSALIENCE - INTUITIVE SMELL

Clairalience, also known as clairscent or clairsentience, involves smelling fragrances or odors of substances, individuals, places, or animals not present. These scents are perceived even if there is no physical reason for the smell, transcending time and space. Often the first scent a person develops is sulfur as a warning sign for a dark entity.

CLAIRTANGENCY - INTUITIVE KNOWING by TOUCHING

Clairtangency, or psychometry, allows a person to touch an object and acquire information about the object, its owner, or its history. It also applies to touching living beings to gain insights.

CLAIRTACTION – INTUITIVE TOUCH

Clairtaction refers to sensing being touched by a spiritual being and knowing information about that spirit. It involves telekinetically extending a touch to both physical and etheric entities, allowing both the recipient and the psychic to be aware of the touch.

CLAIRGUSTANCE – INTUITIVE TASTE

Clairgustance lets a person taste something without physically consuming it. It's a way of experiencing taste without the need for actual consumption.

CLAIREMPATHY – INTUITIVE FEELING of EMOTION

Clairempathy allows individuals to know people and their energies. This ability enables a psychic to experience the thoughts, attitudes, and associated mental, emotional, physical, and spiritual results of a person, place, or animal.

CLAIRELOQUENCE – INTUITIVE COMMUNICATING

Claireloquence is the ability to use precisely the right words to achieve a specific objective. It refers to conveying exact meanings or desired outcomes through words, considering their performative nature and phonology. This can also include channeled communication.

CLAIRESSENCE – INTUITIVE EMBODIMENT

Clairessence is a fundamental and comprehensive intuitive ability. It encompasses Ascension, where understanding it fully renders it insignificant as one becomes "it."

This section of the Document also talked about color theory and healing. Adding more insight, let's briefly explore how color is used and its applications.

RED:

Red, a stimulating color, enhances vitality and energy levels. It's particularly useful for addressing exhaustion, paralysis, or conditions associated with low energy and mobility. By boosting adrenaline, red increases blood flow and pressure. However, it's not suitable for individuals with high blood pressure. Additionally, red stimulates the nervous system, reducing fatigue and preventing common illnesses. It's often associated with gyms and restaurants due to its potential to enhance physical energy. It has been known to create inflammation as well.

MAGENTA:

Magenta is a relaxing color that shares the positive attributes of pink and red. It encourages kindness and cooperation, fostering a sense of self-respect and optimism. Exposure to magenta tends to promote cooperation and positive feelings.

PINK:

Pink, with its nurturing properties, is excellent for emotional healing. It encourages compassion, love, and emotional stability, evoking a calm and soothing ambiance. This high-energy color shares several benefits with red but is less intense. It's a joyful and stimulating color that poses no harm to individuals with high blood pressure. The presence of pink can reduce erratic behavior and promote kindness.

ORANGE:

Orange, a high-energy color, is especially positive for children. It fosters creativity and enthusiasm, providing an energy boost and cultivating a sense of accomplishment. It's particularly beneficial for the immune system, lungs, liver, and spleen. Orange also assists in releasing subconscious constraints and restoring hormonal balance, aiding issues related to fertility and negative energy imbalances.

YELLOW:

Yellow, a cheery and vibrant color, uplifts mood and promotes positivity. Its healing elements encourage positive thoughts and muscle energization. Radiating warmth, yellow relieves depression, fosters optimism, and instills confidence in the healing process. It enhances focus, mental clarity, and digestion while providing sustained energy. Positive thoughts, closely linked to yellow, significantly contribute to healing. Its healing attributes extend to the nervous system, brain stimulation, improved spiritual well-being, and enhanced psychosocial well-being.

LIME:

Lime, a vibrant version of green, boosts activity levels while inducing feelings of safety and security. Being near lime green may enhance immunity.

GREEN:

Green, found abundantly in nature, symbolizes growth and renewal. Its calming influence makes it ideal for meditation and self-reflection. Surroundings rich in green promote relaxation, balance, and unity with nature. Green's healing properties extend to the heart, lungs, and circulatory system. Notably, it corrects hormonal imbalances, aids bacterial issues and infections, and is employed to treat conditions like high blood pressure.

TEAL:

Teal, a fusion of green and blue, instills calmness, clearing negative thoughts and enhancing sleep quality. It offers mental clarity and boosts immunity, making it an excellent color for supporting red blood cell regeneration and preventing infections.

BLUE:

Blue, known for its calming effects, soothes the mind, body, and spirit. Exposure to blue induces relaxation and pain relief, reducing blood pressure and heart rates. It's effective in managing emotions and headaches, while enhancing the senses of smell, sight, and sound. Blue is also known for improving sleep, especially valuable for those struggling with insomnia or restlessness. Its healing attributes are significant. Notably it works to reduce inflammation.

INDIGO:

Indigo amalgamates the positive aspects of purple and blue, broadening perspectives and enhancing intuition. Individuals surrounded by indigo tend to show greater understanding in challenging situations, reducing stress related to health struggles. It instills a sense of peacefulness and is specifically useful for headaches, migraines, and sinus issues. Its healing potential extends to addressing various mental health concerns.

PURPLE:

Purple's healing impact lies in its ability to foster enlightenment and self-awareness. It's an elegant color that promotes relaxation, aiding in stress reduction and better sleep quality. Often used in meditation, purple enhances intuition and supports the immune and nervous systems. Its potential anti-inflammatory properties further contribute to its healing nature.

LAVENDER:

Lavender, a gentle shade of purple, enhances vitality and imparts a sense of youthfulness. It's associated with cleanliness, relaxation, and purity, making it ideal for meditation and reflection. It offers additional healing properties, such as improved sleep and pain reduction.

CREAM:

Cream, akin to white but less glaring, serves as a simple yet welcoming color. It offers control over intense emotions and creates a relaxing environment that contributes to emotional healing.

WHITE:

White, a fusion of all light colors, holds the healing attributes of its counterparts. Symbolizing purity and truth, white prompts reflection, productivity, and mental healing. Physically, it aids recovery from various ailments. Moreover, white promotes conflict resolution and mental well-being, making it a "perfect color" for harmony and balance.

BLACK:

When used thoughtfully, black, though intense, can remove negative energy from one's environment. As it absorbs all colors, black effectively eliminates stressful energy. It reduces anxiety, fosters emotional focus, and assists in processing grief.

BROWN:

Brown, commonly found in nature, signifies stability, reliability, and comfort. It reduces both physical and emotional strain, resulting in enhanced physical strength and reduced stress. Being surrounded by brown can foster a stronger connection to the earth and create a welcoming atmosphere.

31. The Out-of-Body Movement

In the context of The Gateway Process, out-of-body experience is a highly sought-after state and a significant focus of the training. Achieving out-of-body experiences (OBEs) is a goal that many participants hope to attain during their journey at the Monroe Institute.

The technique of achieving OBEs involves reaching a state of expanded awareness, typically starting at Focus 10. Participants are encouraged to relax deeply and synchronize the hemispheres of their brain using Hemi-Sync® sound frequencies. This synchronization allows the individual to enter a state of heightened consciousness, where they become more receptive to exploring dimensions beyond their physical reality.

Once the participant has attained the appropriate state of resonance and relaxation, they are introduced to specific visualization techniques. One such technique involves imagining an "energy balloon," a pattern reminiscent of the cosmic egg, enveloping their entire being. This energy balloon serves as a form of protection against encountering entities with lower energy levels during an OBE.

As the participant continues to advance in their practice and reach deeper states of consciousness, they can explore different focus levels, such as Focus 12 and beyond. Each focus level provides unique opportunities for interaction and self-discovery, and it is within these states that the possibility of out-of-body movement becomes more pronounced.

The Monroe Institute's Gateway Process acknowledges that achieving OBEs can be a gradual and challenging process. Not everyone will experience an OBE immediately or consistently. It requires patience, dedication, and consistent practice with the Hemi-Sync® audios over an extended period.

Ultimately, the objective of The Gateway Process is to empower participants to explore and interact with expanded states of consciousness, including OBEs, for personal growth and self-discovery. While the experience of OBEs may vary among individuals, the training aims to open doors to new dimensions of awareness and understanding beyond the confines of physical reality.

ORIGINAL CIA REPORT SUMMARY AND OVERVIEW:

The topic of out-of-body movement is a subject of great interest within The Gateway Process, but it is not the sole purpose of the program, nor is it guaranteed that all participants will achieve it during their training at the Monroe Institute. Out-of-body experiences (OBEs) are discussed later in the program and are explored in depth in one of the audios.

The techniques for achieving OBEs are designed to facilitate the process for individuals whose brainwave patterns and personal energy levels have reached a point where they are ready for potential separation from the physical body. The Hemi-Sync® tape used for this technique employs Beta signals around 2877.3 cycles per second (CPS). Considering that 30 to 40 CPS is the normal range for Beta brainwave signals associated with the wakeful state, the Monroe Institute believes that this heightened state of brainwave frequency output aids in promoting altered states of consciousness and facilitates the attainment of out-of-body states.

The actual techniques for separating from the body are relatively simple maneuvers, such as rolling out, lifting out headfirst as if sliding up a telephone pole, or sliding out through either end of the body. These techniques are intended to be practiced when the individual feels they have reached a suitable state of resonance and relaxation.

It is important to note that achieving an out-of-body state requires patience, dedication, and practice. It is not always an immediate or consistent experience for everyone. The Monroe Institute emphasizes that The Gateway Process offers a comprehensive approach to exploring expanded states of consciousness and personal growth, and while out-of-body movement is a fascinating aspect, it is just one part of the broader journey of self-discovery and understanding.

SUMMARY AND ADDITIONS:

Exactly, achieving an out-of-body experience (OBE) is not guaranteed for every participant in The Gateway Process. Even if a person completes the training, they may not have an OBE experience. It is important for readers to understand that the program offers tools and techniques to explore expanded states of consciousness, including the potential for OBEs, but the outcome may vary for each individual.

The audios and techniques provided in The Gateway Experience can certainly aid in facilitating the possibility of an OBE, but achieving this state consciously on one's own may require years of dedicated practice and exploration. The key is to continue the practice and work towards this state, recognizing that progress and experiences may come at different rates for each person. The journey of self-discovery and exploration of consciousness is a personal and ongoing process, and patience and persistence are essential elements in developing such skills and abilities.

32. Role of REM Sleep

Mr. Monroe claims that one of his former trainers utilized the Hemi-Sync® Program in conjunction with an induced state of rapid eye movement (REM) and, with this combination, guarantees his students an out-of-body experience (OBE).

ORIGINAL CIA REPORT SUMMARY AND OVERVIEW:

It is worth noting that Bob Monroe informed the Gateway class on May 7, 1983, that an ex-trainer of his working in Charlottesville, Virginia discovered a technique to guarantee out-of-body experiences (OBE) by putting participants into a REM state of sleep and then using the Hemi-Sync® tape technique. This could be because most, if not all, people are said to go into an out-of-body state during REM sleep.

EM sleep is the deepest level of sleep possible, involving complete disengagement of the body's motor cortex functions from the neck down and nearly complete suppression of consciousness in the left brain hemisphere. This induces a state of complete stillness in terms of the skeletal muscle structure, promoting the deep rest required to eliminate the bifurcation echo. Additionally, it frees up the right hemisphere of the brain to respond to the instructions and suggestions on the Gateway tape.

However, using the Hemi-Sync® audios at this point may be more about focusing the brain enough so that a residual memory of having naturally achieved an out-of-body state is carried into the waking state rather than actually achieving the out-of-body state. Some dreams associated with deep levels of sleep may be functions of the same type of altered consciousness involved in interaction with the universe, similar to all the Focus 12, 15, and 21 states described above.

The difference between those states and the state of mind in REM sleep appears to be that the left hemisphere is almost completely disengaged in the latter experience, such that memory of what was accomplished in the altered states of consciousness cannot usually be retrieved by conscious desire because the left hemisphere has no knowledge of its own existence or location in the right hemisphere. Although some people can be

162

trained to remember their REM state dreams through intense conditioning in the waking state, this may be due to the right hemisphere establishing pathways that the left hemisphere can access following reentry into the wakeful state, rather than any specific left hemisphere conscious involvement in the process during REM sleep.

In any event, the three apparent conditions required for voluntarily inducing an out-of-body state in most individuals seem to be:

1. *Achievement of a state of profound quiet in the body, such that the bifurcation echo fades and resonance at approximately seven Hertz is established.*

2. *Synchronization of the two brain hemisphere wave patterns.*

3. *Subsequent stimulation of the right hemisphere of the mind to attain a state of heightened alertness (which, of course, interferes with brain hemisphere synchronization but not until a sufficient level of enhanced frequency range has first been established to help achieve the out-of-body state).*

SUMMARY AND ADDITIONS:

While there was no mention of specific studies or the identity of the former trainer, it is understood that REM sleep typically occurs about ninety minutes after falling asleep. During this stage, your eyes move rapidly from side to side behind closed eyelids. Brain wave activity becomes mixed frequency and closer to that seen in wakefulness. Breathing becomes faster and irregular, while heart rate and blood pressure increase to near waking levels. Most dreaming occurs during REM sleep, although some can also happen during non-REM sleep. Additionally, your arm and leg muscles become temporarily paralyzed during this stage, preventing you from acting out your dreams. As you age, the time spent in REM sleep decreases. Memory consolidation likely requires both non-REM and REM sleep.

To achieve an out-of-body experience (OBE), three essential conditions must be present: profound quietness in the body and resonance at seven hertz, synchronized hemispheres of the brain, and stimulation of the right brain. The crucial distinction lies in the stimulation of the right brain rather than just having access to it.

33. Information Collection Potential

The science and application as taught and used at The Monroe Institute have encountered some challenges. While several students have been able to achieve the level of practice required for out-of-body travel and remote viewing, the accuracy of the information gathered in these states was found to be less than ideal.

ORIGINAL CIA REPORT SUMMARY AND OVERVIEW:

From the standpoint of developing practical applications for the Gateway technique, the information acquisition potential associated with the out-of-body state appears to attract the most attention.

Unfortunately, although the out-of-body state can be achieved, the purposes to which it can be put are currently limited by the fact that although individuals in that state may travel anywhere on an instantaneous basis in either the terrestrial or in other spheres, information distortion in the former context remains a major concern.

Several experiments have been conducted to date, according to one of the Monroe Institute's trainers, involving people moving from one coast to the other in an out-of-body state to read a series of ten computer-generated numbers in a university laboratory. Although most have learned enough of the digits to demonstrate that their consciousness was present, no one has ever gotten all ten correct.

This appears to be because physical reality in the present is not the only holographic influence that an individual may encounter while out-of-body. There are also energy patterns left by people or events that occurred at the same physical location being viewed in the past rather than the present. Furthermore, because thoughts are the product of energy patterns, and energy patterns are reality, it is possible that individuals may encounter thought forms while in an out-of-body state that blend

166

with physical reality and are difficult to distinguish.

Finally, as Melissa Jager writes, there is another potential problem area in the sense that holograms can be viewed. Pseudoascetically, that is, inside out or backward, they can be seen in proper perspective. Some of the distortions that occur may eventually be traceable to this cause because an individual in an out-of-body state may perceive the holographic energy patterns given off by people or things interacting in time-space reality in a somewhat distorted form.

SUMMARY AND ADDITIONS:

Additional research from the CIA access portal indicates that Project Grill Flame, later coined Center Lane, used The Gateway Project as a basis for developing remote viewing intelligence gathering. In their research, dozens of tests were conducted, and approximately 50 percent of them produced useful and actionable data. One notable project involved locating a missing airplane. However, the project on its own never proved to be consistently effective but rather an expensive endeavor. Therefore, if someone were to use this method of data collection, it would be crucial to conduct experiments that can easily be verified as true or false and work towards creating accurate results before making any truth claims.

Holograms pose a challenge, and although we may access and comprehend other dimensions, times, and places through viewing these holograms, we must consider the potential for errors in perception. It is essential to approach such experiences with a critical mindset and be aware of the complexities involved in interpreting holographic information.

34. Belief System Considerations

In the following section, McDonnell addresses the concern that the discovery or method described in the Gateway Project could potentially disrupt any particular religion. However, he finds that all religions, in their own way, point to or tie in with the same underlying philosophy. McDonnell points out that mystics from various religious groups have carried this same knowledge of what he refers to as the Absolute, indicating a common thread of understanding among different spiritual traditions.

ORIGINAL CIA REPORT SUMMARY AND OVERVIEW:

In 1967, Alexandra David-Neel and Llama Yongden authored a book entitled "Secret Oral Teachings in Tibetan Buddhist Sects," from which the following quote is taken: "The tangible world is movement, say the Masters, not a collection of moving objects, but movement itself. There are no objects in motion," it is the movement that creates the objects we see: they are nothing but movement.

This movement is a never-ending and infinitely fast succession of flashes of energy (in Tibetan, "tsal" or "shoug"). All perceptible objects to our senses, all phenomena of whatever kind and aspect they may take, are made up of a rapid succession of instantaneous events."

The classic description of the universal hologram is to be found in a Hindu sutra which says: "In the heaven of Indra there is said to be a network of pearls so arranged that if you look at one you see all the others reflected in it."

This quotation has been cited because it demonstrates that the concept of the universe that at least some physicists are now coming to accept is fundamentally identical to the one known to the learned elite in selected civilizations and cultures of high attainment in the ancient world. Scholars familiar with ancient writings of eastern religions, for example, are familiar with the concept of the cosmic egg.

Nor are the theories presented in this paper at variance with the essential tenets of the Judeo-Christian stream of thought.

170

The concept of visible reality (i.e., the "created" world) as an emanation of an omnipotent and omniscient divinity who, in his primary state of being, is completely unknowable. The concept of the Absolute at rest in infinity comes straight from Hebrew mystical philosophy. Even the Christian concept of the Trinity shines through this paper's description of the Absolute.

The description of energy totally at rest, in infinity fits the Christian metaphysical concept of the Father while the infinite self-consciousness resident in that energy providing the motive force of will bring a portion of that energy into motion to create reality corresponds with the Son. This is because, to achieve self-consciousness, the Absolute's consciousness must project a hologram of itself and then perceive it. That hologram is a mirror image of the Absolute in infinity, still exists outside time and space, but is one step removed from the Absolute and is the actual agent of all creation (all reality). And the eternal thought or concept of self which results from this self-consciousness serves the… (continued)

The original document was missing page 25, and page 24 ended abruptly. However, the missing page has now been recovered and is included in this summary.

PREVIOUSLY MISSING "PAGE 25" OF DOCUMENT

The missing page (page 25) includes the conclusion of part 34 and covers part 35 and 36. These sections will be summarized together as one section for author additions.

The concept of the Absolute as the central force around which the evolution of time-space revolves, leading to a reflection in union with it, aligns with the Christian metaphysical description of the Holy Spirit. The idea of a thought model perfectly reflecting the essence of the Absolute resonates with the concept of the Holy Spirit in Christian philosophy.

Additionally, the depiction of the universal hologram, representing the Taurus of creation and evolution, is not a novel idea. It has been present in various stylized forms across numerous religious systems, both Eastern and Western. From the stylized labyrinth of the Hellenic world to the spiralized versions of the Hebrew tree of life, its Hindu counterpart, or the Chinese spiral through the fourfold powers, the ultimate meaning remains consistent. Mystics worldwide seem to have perceived the universal hologram in the same spiral form and have integrated this intuitive knowledge into their religious writings from ancient times to the present.

35. Left brain limitations.

In the 20th century, physics seems to be revisiting insights that have been present in human understanding for as long as written records can be traced. The difference lies in the approach taken by 20th-century physics, which primarily employs a left brain, linear, and quantitative style of reasoning. On the other hand, the Mystics of old seemingly acquired the same knowledge through a holistic, intuitive, right brain style of perception.

172

The Gateway process appears to be a promising tool in our left brain culture, as it offers a potential method for achieving the intuitive and holistic interference with the universal hologram. Thinkers like Einstein, who sought to discover a unified field theory in physics, sought this context. Access to a new world of intuitive perception and self-reflection could provide a pathway to genuine objectivity for professionals dealing with strategic issues, tactical questions, and matters of managerial form and system.

Our culture and personal psychological subjectivity often impose limitations on balanced perception and objective logic when we rely solely on the left brain thinking style. However, the holistic form of perception associated with altered states of consciousness might counteract these limitations. By fully perceiving ourselves in the context of our reflection within the universal hologram, we may free ourselves from the constraints of subjectivity.

36. Self-knowledge.

The ancient Mystic philosophers emphasized the importance of "Know thyself" as the first step toward personal maturity. They believed that education should begin with achieving an introverted focus, understanding what lies within oneself before engaging with the outside world. Their insight was accurate in recognizing that one must comprehend their own psychological balance before effectively evaluating and coping with the world.

Twentieth-century philosophy, with its various personality testing methods, seemed to rekindle this ancient intuition. However, no personality test can replace the depth of self-perception that can be attained when the mind alters its state of consciousness enough to perceive its own hologram projected onto the universe. This holistic and intuitive perception of oneself as part of the universal hologram is unparalleled.

The Gateway experience holds the promise of providing a portal through which individuals, after months or even years of practice, may embark on a journey of self-discovery, personal effectiveness, and truth in a broader sense. It offers the potential for profound self-awareness and understanding, which can lead to a deeper connection with the universal order.

SUMMARY AND ADDITIONS:

These three sections, Belief systems, Left Brain Limitations, and Self-Knowledge, all converge on a common truth. Throughout history, various sources, including religions, intuitives, mystics, and modern scientists, have all hinted at the same underlying reality – that we, along with all matter and space we perceive, form a universal hologram.

What was once considered a mere belief system based on human creation is now finding validation through scientific exploration. Our pursuit of a deeper truth has led us to discover the reality of the Absolute, not because we intended to scientifically prove it, but because our quest for understanding has reshaped our perception.

Furthermore, by undertaking introspection and sincere study, we can come to realize that we are holographic reflections of the whole. The Gateway Process provides an accessible path to attaining this knowledge. Ultimately, the purpose of life seems to be the age-old adage, "to know thyself."

37. Motivational Aspect

The world we live in today often lacks patience, and it is no surprise that we have developed a process that aligns with our desire for immediate results. Drawing from our scientific understanding of how the brain and body function, we have devised a method to accelerate our comprehension of life's complexities.

In this fast-paced world, the Hemi-Sync® audios cater to our need for instant gratification. McDonnell astutely recognizes the significance of emphasizing this aspect for the readers of the report.

ORIGINAL CIA REPORT SUMMARY AND OVERVIEW:

The Gateway process is a step-by-step procedure involving repetitive practice of the techniques. Each new insight obtained during the practice serves as a means of delving deeper in subsequent sessions. Interestingly, the Gateway approach appears to advance at a much faster pace compared to transcendental meditation or other forms of mental self-discipline. Its scope extends far beyond, making it accessible even to individuals in our impatient, result-oriented, and skeptical society.

Unlike yoga and certain other eastern mental disciplines, Gateway does not demand infinite patience or total personal subservience to a lifelong system of discipline. It starts yielding at least minimal results within a relatively short period, providing feedback that motivates and energizes the individual to continue practicing.

The rate of progress in Gateway seems to depend less on the number of hours spent practicing and more on how quickly one can apply the insights gained to alleviate anxieties and stresses in both mind and body. Energy blockages in these areas are the primary hindrances to achieving enhanced energy states and mental focus required for swift advancement. Initially, individuals who are more compulsive or tense may encounter more barriers in attaining deep or immediate experiences. However, as insights arise and blockages dissolve, the path ahead becomes clearer, and the value of Gateway transforms from

*intellectual assessment to personal
experience.*

SUMMARY AND ADDITIONS:

The Gateway process offers a significant advantage in accessing our innate self-knowledge by creating a feedback mechanism that serves as strong motivation to continue. Unlike engaging in a lifelong practice of transcendental meditation, which may take years before reaching the levels that The Gateway Process opens, the Gateway approach offers a faster timeline and more frequent intervals of success. This accelerated progress and the regular experiences of success encourage participants to persist with enthusiasm.

The knowledge that even after years of dedication, traditional practices may only offer a chance of possibility can deter many individuals from even starting. However, with the Gateway Process, the quicker results and the consistent sense of accomplishment foster a sense of determination and dedication to continue the journey of self-discovery. The regular feedback loop becomes a driving force, propelling participants forward on their path of exploration and growth.

38. Conclusion

ORIGINAL CIA REPORT SUMMARY AND OVERVIEW:

The Gateway Experience presents a rational basis within the parameters of physical science, making it plausible in achieving essential objectives. Intuitive insights, both on a personal and professional level, are well within reasonable expectations.

To accelerate progress and make the Gateway process more manageable, a phased approach is recommended for organization-wide adoption:

A. Begin with the Gateway Hemi-Sync® audios to enhance brain focus and induce hemisphere synchronization.

B. Incorporate strong REM sleep frequencies for left brain inactivity and deep physical relaxation.

C. Provide hypnotic suggestions for inducing deep autohypnotic states at will.

D. Use autohypnotic suggestions for improved focus and motivation during Focus 12 exercises.

E. Revisit steps A and B, using autohypnotic suggestion to induce and remember out-of-body experiences.

F. Practice and gain control over conscious out-of-body movement using hypnotic suggestion.

G. Approach Focus 15 and 21 objectives from the out-of-body perspective.

H. Implement a multi-focus approach for overcoming distortion in terrestrial information gathering trips with three individuals in the out-of-body state.

I. Encourage self-knowledge to enhance objectivity and remove personal energy blockages hindering progress.

J. Be intellectually prepared for encounters with non-corporal energy forms beyond time-space boundaries.

K. Form groups in Focus 12 state to build holographic patterns around sensitive areas to repel unwanted out-of-body presences.

L. Advanced Gateway participants should create holographic patterns of success to assist colleagues in progressing through the Gateway system.

By conducting these experiments and following the proposed approach, it is hoped that Gateway will open the door to practical application and unleash the full potential of its techniques for all participants.

SUMMARY AND ADDITIONS:

McDonnell's recommendation to the US Army Intelligence and Security Command was to conduct experiments with multiple agents simultaneously to increase the chances of obtaining accurate results. This is because in some cases, it might be challenging to determine if a person is receiving a clear holographic perspective.

This practice can also be applied to personal practice. Creating a group of like-minded friends and practicing with the same targets at the same time allows for comparison of travel notes. Alternatively, having someone who can validate the results adds credibility to the findings.

However, it is crucial to exercise caution when disclosing or relying on findings until there is confidence in their accuracy. Practice and time are essential to refine the abilities and interpretations.

Desiree M. Palmer

Overview of the Hemi-Sync® Audios

As we delve deeper into this profound exploration, it becomes evident that the Gateway Experience is not a one-size-fits-all endeavor. Each participant brings to the table a unique set of abilities, life experiences, and perspectives. This individuality is at the core of the Gateway, as it is precisely tailored to suit each participant's needs and objectives.

It is imperative, however, to acknowledge that this journey may not always proceed without challenges. There will inevitably be moments of uncertainty, confusion, and, at times, frustration. Yet, it is crucial to recognize that these are often the very moments that mark the precipice of a significant breakthrough. This journey can be likened to ascending a mountain: while the view from the summit is awe-inspiring, the ascent demands unwavering effort and perseverance.

Think of it as a hike up a mountain, You may find yourself in sheer awe of the grandeur of nature. Each step prompting reflections on how this physical journey mirrors our collective quest for self-discovery. The path, characterized by its twists and turns, much like the intricacies of our consciousness as we navigate the quest, it becomes a metaphor for exploration.

However, it is vital to emphasize that the true essence of this journey does not solely reside in reaching the summit. The genuine beauty of this experience lies in the journey itself—the encounters, the self-realizations, and the continuous growth. Every step taken, every experience encountered, brings us closer to understanding our own inner truths.

186

Consider this proposition: What if we approached life with the same openness and curiosity that we bring to the Gateway Experience? What if we permitted ourselves to embrace the unknown, welcome uncertainty, and relinquish the need for definitive answers?

Life, in its essence, is a journey—one filled with unexpected twists and turns. It is in these unanticipated detours that some of the most profound lessons emerge. Thus, as you embark on this odyssey of self-discovery, I encourage you to maintain an open heart and mind. Embrace the allure of the unknown, for it shall serve as your guide to the uncharted territories of consciousness.

While engaging with the Hemi-Sync® audios, you will discern how they gently facilitate your transition into a state of deep relaxation and heightened awareness. This experience is akin to embarking on a meditative journey with a trusted companion by your side. These audios are thoughtfully designed to be your supportive ally on this voyage, rather than an overwhelming force.

Furthermore, it is worth noting that as you venture deeper into the Gateway, you will come to realize that this journey is perpetual. It is a lifelong expedition, an eternal unfolding of the self. This, in essence, is where the enchantment lies—we are infinite beings, in a state of perpetual evolution and discovery.

Let us raise a symbolic toast to the boundless potential within each of us. Let us celebrate the art of introspection, the joy of storytelling, and the profound power of connection. Above all, let us celebrate YOU—an extraordinary individual endowed with the ability to tap into the universal hologram.

Are you prepared to take the next step? Are you eager to unravel the enigma of your consciousness and embrace the vast cosmos within you? I certainly am, and I am eager to accompany you on this journey.

So, as we continue this shared adventure, let us wholeheartedly immerse ourselves, let us explore with unwavering curiosity, and let us embrace the wonder that awaits us. The Gateway Experience beckons—are you ready to respond to its call? Let us embark on this journey with enthusiasm, determination, and a sense of purpose. Let us proceed.

In the beginning

Step one is all about embracing the truth that you are so much more than just a physical body and a human mind. You are an energetic being, and this realization is the foundation of your journey into the Gateway Experience. So, let's start by being an observer – observing the differences within ourselves without making judgments.

Imagine this: different Hemi-Sync® audio techniques produce unique brain wave patterns, and these differences can be perceived differently within you. How fascinating is that? Let's tune in and feel these differences kinesthetically – pay close attention to the subtle sensations your body generates. It's like riding the waves at the edge of the ocean, feeling the rise and fall, the rocking, and the sliding.

And here's a reminder – language is a visual concept. We often admire those who have insight or can see into the future. But beware, your ego may create false visions just to make you believe you're succeeding in the process. It's like creating a beautiful sandcastle at the beach – a sight to behold, but remember, it's just foam on the surface, not the true strength of the ocean.

But fear not, my friend! Visualizations can be powerful, and while it may be difficult to know what's genuine and what's made up, trust the process. Keep a journal of your experiences and how they make you feel. These subtleties help you grow your perception muscle, leading to clearer visions and deeper understandings.

In this journey, there's no right or wrong way to participate. Delve deep into yourself, appreciate more of what's around you, and value your individuality within the wholeness and unity of the experience.

Now, let's talk about correlation messages. Mediums train themselves to receive messages by creating their own unique connections. It's like forming a bank of symbols and meanings – when they see a red balloon, it might indicate a birthday celebration.

So, consider these questions and write down the first thing that comes to mind – your key to correlation messages:

What represents fear to you?

What represents money to you?

What represents celebration to you?

What represents betrayal to you?

What represents love to you?

What represents hard work to you?

What represents fun to you?

What represents regret to you?

And continue with your own questions...

Creating your unique symbols and interpretations will help you navigate the messages you receive during your journey. Let me share an example – I once saw a snake lodged in someone's spine, and my immediate assumption was that it was a dark attachment. But, in reality, it represented fear – something I personally fear. Understanding this helped the person release the fear stuck in their sacral chakra, and it wasn't a dark entity as I initially thought.

So, my friend, let's equip ourselves with this guide of images and interpretations to better understand the messages we receive during our journey through the Gateway Experience. It's a personal adventure filled with self-discovery and growth. Are you ready to dive in? Let's embark on this extraordinary quest together!

Focus Levels Explained

Let's delve into the Focus Levels – a system of signposts designed by Monroe to expand our consciousness. These levels showcase various states of awareness, like global consciousness or specific individual awareness. But remember, they're more like guides than rigid destinations. Your journey is unique, so let it unfold naturally. The audio program introduces these Focus Levels briefly, leaving room for your own exploration. According to my research, Focus 10 was the starting point, and the other levels were developed from there. No strict rules, just a fascinating journey of understanding consciousness through these Focus Levels.

I have included a summary of any Focus levels I could find information on and their definitions.

FOCUS I
FULL, PHYSICAL WAKING CONSCIOUSNESS

Focus 1 is the realm of everyday reality where we all live and experience life. It's often referred to as

Conscious 1 (C-1) because it's the state of awareness we're most familiar with during our waking hours. In Focus 1, we are fully immersed in the physical world, completely identified with both form and Ego. But guess what? This is precisely the level of consciousness we aim to transcend through this training.

FOCUS 3
INCREASED MENTAL COHERENCY AND BALANCE

At Focus 3, participants are introduced to the fascinating world of Hemi-Sync® and its transformative technology. It's a level where relaxation and heightened awareness become attainable, marking the beginning of a profound journey towards enlightenment.

In a way, Focus 3 can be likened to a stepping stone towards the realm of 4D or higher consciousness. Here, we start to loosen our identification with the physical form and ego, but we haven't fully immersed ourselves in the depths of higher awareness just yet.

It's essential to acknowledge that, as humans, we are inherently rooted in Focus 1, our everyday reality. However, as we progress through this transformative process, we find ourselves experiencing fleeting moments in other focus levels. As our enlightenment flourishes, these glimpses into other dimensions become more frequent, drawing us closer to the realms beyond Focus 1.

FOCUS 10
MIND AWAKE/BODY ASLEEP

Focus 10, a fascinating state where the physical body slumbers, yet the mind remains fully awake and aware of its surroundings. Here, consciousness is not reliant on signals from the physical form. It's a unique realm where we can stay fully conscious even as our body rests.

In Focus 10, we are equipped with powerful conceptual tools that can be harnessed for various purposes. These tools help us reduce anxiety, alleviate tension, facilitate healing, practice remote sensing, and connect with others through resonance. They prove to be invaluable in navigating diverse situations.

In this state, our thought processes shift, and we find ourselves thinking in vivid images rather than words—almost akin to experiencing a dream state while being fully aware. Interestingly, a small percentage of individuals might find it challenging to move beyond Focus 1. They may struggle to visualize, imagine, dream, or recall images in their minds, firmly anchored in the physical form and ego. Rest assured, this is a rare occurrence, and most people can develop their ability to explore other focus levels with practice and dedication. So, fear not, for as you work with the process, your capacity to delve deeper into the realms of consciousness will undoubtedly expand.

FOCUS 12
EXPANDED AWARENESS

In Focus 12, we transcend the limitations of our physical body and venture into nonphysical realities, opening a world of possibilities. It's like stepping into a realm of expanded awareness where decision-making, problem-solving, and creativity are taken to new heights. The power of this level lies in its ability to unlock hidden abilities within us.

So, how do we access this transcendent state? In my personal experience, the key is curiosity. Embrace your curiosity and let it guide you. Perhaps you have a burning question or a challenging problem to solve. In the state of Focus 12, be curious about the answers. Be open to exploring other dimensions and be ready to receive new perceptions and ideas.

When I'm in this state, I notice that the thoughts and ideas I receive are unlike anything I've thought of before. They seem to come from somewhere beyond my conscious mind. The more curious and open I remain, the deeper and more profound the insights become. It's as if the universe is revealing its secrets to me, one revelation at a time.

However, there's a catch. The moment I start analyzing or overthinking these insights, the flow stops. It's like trying to grasp water in your hands - the tighter you hold, the more it slips away. Instead, I've learned to trust the process and let the information come to me naturally.

Focus 12 offers a gateway to new levels of growth and development. As we explore nonphysical realities with curiosity and an open mind, we tap into a vast reservoir of knowledge and wisdom. It's an exhilarating journey of self-discovery and understanding, and the possibilities are limitless. So, let your curiosity be your guide, and let the revelations unfold in their own time. You'll be amazed at what you can discover when you embrace the transcendent state of Focus 12.

FOCUS 15
NO TIME

Welcome to Focus 15, the realm of "No Time" - a state of consciousness that transcends the limitations of time and space. Here, the mind opens up to endless opportunities for self-exploration, unrestricted by the confines of linear time. It's like stepping into the void of pure potentiality.

In this state, consciousness moves far beyond the signals transmitted by the physical body. Time becomes irrelevant as experiences are no longer bound by a linear sequence. It's as if you enter a timeless dimension where past, present, and future blend together in a harmonious dance.

Think of it as the ultimate "no mind" state, similar to the practice of some Buddhist traditions. Here, the mind is free from the incessant chatter of thoughts. It's a state of pure being, where you are not actively creating thoughts but rather observing the flow of existence.

Now, achieving this state on your own, without the aid of Hemi-Sync® audios, can be quite challenging. It requires a profound level of mastery and discipline. But fear not, with the help of Hemi-Sync® audios, we can venture into this realm of pure potentiality with greater ease.

In Focus 15, you have the opportunity to tap into the boundless wisdom and insights that reside in this timeless void. It's a realm of limitless possibilities, where you can gain profound understandings about yourself and the universe.

So, let go of the constraints of time and space. Embrace the emptiness of the "No Time" state and allow yourself to be in perfect harmony with the universe. As you delve into this realm of pure potential, you'll discover a profound sense of peace and oneness that transcends all limitations. Prepare to embark on a journey of self-discovery unlike anything you've experienced before. The path to Focus 15 may be challenging, but the rewards are immeasurable. Embrace the void and unlock the secrets of the universe within.

FOCUS 21
OTHER ENERGY SYSTEMS

Focus 21, the realm of Alternate Realities and Infinite Energy Systems! Here, the boundaries of time, space, and physical matter dissolve, allowing you to explore realms beyond the limitations of our ordinary reality. It's like standing on the threshold of the time/space continuum, where your mind remains fully conscious and active.

Unlike the gradual progression we experienced in the earlier levels, Focus 21 is a state that cannot be willed into existence. Instead, it's a realm that you stumble upon or spontaneously pop into from seemingly nowhere. It's as if the universe opens up to reveal its hidden dimensions, and you find yourself immersed in a vast expanse of boundless possibilities.

You might wonder if accessing this level is reserved for gifted individuals like mediums, psychics, or intuitives. But here's the thrilling revelation: we all have access to all focus levels at any given time. Think about a medium communicating with departed spirits (Focus 27), a psychic foreseeing the future (Focus 21), or an intuitive who spontaneously grasps an answer to a question (Focus 12). These abilities are not confined to a select few; they are inherent within all of us.

The Gateway training doesn't bestow upon us new powers; instead, it empowers us to unlock and harness the latent potentials we already possess. Through dedicated practice and guided by the Hemi-Sync® audios, we can deliberately venture into these extraordinary realms of consciousness.

In Focus 21, you are invited to delve into alternate realities, where the possibilities are limitless. It's an adventure of a lifetime, one that takes you beyond the constraints of our everyday reality. Embrace the serendipity of this exploration, for you never know what wonders await you in the vast landscape of alternate realities and infinite energy systems.

So, open your mind and heart to the unknown. Allow yourself to be carried into the depths of Focus 21, where the fabric of reality is woven with threads of pure potential. With each step you take, you'll uncover new dimensions of existence and come to realize that the universe is far grander and more interconnected than we ever imagined.

FOCUS 22
COMATOSE

Focus 22, the threshold between physical and nonphysical modes of existence! Here, you are teetering on the edge of a profound transition, where the boundaries between the material world and the ethereal realms blur into one another. It's a state that offers a unique perspective on the nature of consciousness and existence.

Focus 22 has been described by Robert Monroe as a comatose state, reminiscent of the altered states induced by certain illicit drugs. In this realm, the mind is in a profoundly altered state of consciousness, where the usual perceptions of reality are distorted and expanded. It's like being in a dreamlike state, where the boundaries between the inner world of the mind and the external world of the senses become fluid.

In this enigmatic state, you may find yourself witnessing the interplay of energies and dimensions beyond the physical realm. It's a realm of heightened awareness, where the veils that separate us from the mysteries of the universe are temporarily lifted.

While the comparison to comatose or drug-induced states may sound daunting, it's essential to remember that the Gateway training offers a safe and guided way to explore these altered states of consciousness. Unlike drug-induced experiences, which can be unpredictable and potentially harmful, the Gateway process is carefully designed to provide a controlled and purposeful journey.

Embrace the potential of Focus 22 as an opportunity to gain profound insights into the nature of reality and consciousness. As you navigate the delicate balance between physical and nonphysical existence, you may come to realize that our understanding of reality is but a mere fraction of the grand tapestry of existence.

Allow yourself to let go of preconceived notions and open your mind to the vast mysteries that lie beyond our ordinary perception. Remember, in Focus 22, you are at the threshold of profound discovery, where the limitations of our physical world give way to the boundless realms of the nonphysical. So, step forward with curiosity and courage, and let the mysteries of Focus 22 unfold before you. The journey continues!

FOCUS 23
"NEW ARRIVALS"

A realm where the energies of souls who have departed from their physical existence but have not yet transcended to their full energetic selves reside. In this unique space, these souls find themselves in a state of transition, not fully returning to the oneness of the spiritual realm.

Imagine a place where energies seem to be "stuck," hovering between the physical and nonphysical worlds, often confused and unaware of their current state. They may not even realize that they have passed on from their physical life, continuing to seek contact with the familiar people and places they once knew.

As they cling to the remnants of their physical existence, they are hesitant to let go and embrace the next phase of their journey. In this limbo, they are not yet ready to move on to the higher planes of existence, holding onto the ties that bind them to the physical plane.

When a medium encounters a soul in this state, it is on the plane of Focus 23 where they meet. In his teachings, Robert Monroe mentions the existence of guides specifically tasked with assisting these souls on their path to transition. However, due to their strong attachment to the physical plane, these souls may struggle to connect with their guides and find their way forward.

However, a significant aspect of this focus is the opportunity it provides for physical beings, like mediums or those with the gift of communication with the nonphysical, to lend a helping hand. When they encounter a soul that has not yet moved on, they can serve as a bridge between the departed soul and their guides, facilitating their journey to the next phase of existence.

It is a profound and compassionate act to guide these souls toward their ultimate destination, helping them release their ties to the physical world and embrace the greater reality that awaits them. In this interconnected realm of Focus 23, the transition between worlds becomes a shared journey, where the physical and nonphysical unite to aid those in need of guidance.

As you explore Focus 23, allow your heart to open to the plight of these souls, and let your compassion become a guiding light for their way forward. It is a space where understanding and assistance meet, where energies intertwine to find solace and resolution. Embrace this remarkable opportunity to be a conduit for their journey as you continue your exploration of the Gateway.

FOCUS 24, 25, 26
BELIEF SYSTEM TERRITORIES (BST)

Focus 24, 25, and 26—a trio of profound realms where the rich tapestry of belief systems unfolds. Picture them as unique heavens, each distinct and abundant in its own way, much like diverse spiritual traditions that have flourished throughout human history. In these realms, individual energies intermingle, connected by shared ideas and ideologies, forming a collective tapestry of beliefs.

It's essential to keep in mind that these Focus areas are not the destinations themselves but signposts guiding us towards the expansive realms of the absolute. They are gateways to states of consciousness beyond the traditional program, offering a profound focus on service—service both to those existing in our physical reality and to those who have transitioned from the physical and may benefit from our assistance.

In the physical realm, we discover the art of sending healing energy to those who seek it, while in the energetic realm, we delve into the wonders of Focus Levels 23 to 27, aiming ultimately to reach Focus 27, the transcendent state.

Exploring the BST entails a deep dive into our current beliefs and operating structures in the world. As curiosity guides us, we question our most limiting beliefs and how our present ideologies support our desire for uninhibited exploration.

While these activities are often associated with "rescue and retrieval," the most profound impact arises from the personal revelations we encounter along the way. Assisting others on their journey often leads us to retrieve lost parts of ourselves, fostering a sense of wholeness, completion, and inner harmony. This is also where ancestral work takes place, connecting us to our roots and inherited wisdom.

At times, our journey serves as a mirror, reflecting back insights, experiences, and connections that might initially seem unrelated but reveal deeper layers of understanding.

Focus 24 welcomes us to a safe haven of non-physical energies, nurturing cultural and religious ideologies. This is where concepts are stored, identified, and explored, manifesting in diverse belief systems.

In Focus 25, we encounter the intricate web of religious structures, emerging from this realm and encompassing all current and practiced spiritual systems. It encompasses beliefs that embrace or exclude a higher being, encompassing everything from Catholicism to Buddhism, and even ideologies like Atheism.

Focus 26, on the other hand, is a space for thinkers and visionaries, where singular spiritual belief systems find their understanding. Those have direct experiences or develop their own profound insights reside here. It's a realm of individual spiritual seekers, like Buddha, Christ, or lesser-known mystics and philosophers whose ideas go beyond commonly held religious or group understandings.

In essence, the BST houses the core of our spiritual identity, a place where our beliefs reside, express, and evolve. Journeying through these realms opens doors to profound self-discovery, as we unravel the vast tapestry of human beliefs and ideologies, and perhaps uncover a deeper understanding of our own spiritual path.

FOCUS 27
THE PARK

Focus 27, the state of "being" or exploration known as *The Park*! Here, something extraordinary awaits—communication with foreign intelligences from all corners of the cosmos, gathered to observe the happenings on our dear Earth. It's like a cosmic symposium of beings, converging to witness the unfolding events on our beloved planet.

Monroe, in his book Far Journeys, unraveled this fascinating realm, where encounters with alien intelligences are within reach. And what's even more remarkable is that this state, The Park offers a more efficient way to collect memories. Imagine remembering countless intricate details of your entire experience—it's like having a limitless memory bank!

But let me offer a little side note: Focus 27 marks the limit of the Earth Life System (ELS). While you can encounter non-human intelligences in various levels, beyond Focus 27 is the domain of the non-human, non-Earth-based life forms, both physical and beyond the physical.

FOCUS 34 & 35
THE GATHERING

Focus 34 and 35—a realm that unveils the Earth's waystation, a pivotal hub in our vast universe. Just as every civilization possesses its unique waystation, Earth boasts its own, known as The Gathering.

As described in Monroe's book, "Far Journeys," The Gathering serves as a state of being, enabling communication with foreign intelligences from distant realms, commonly referred to as "aliens." These enigmatic beings have convened here to keenly observe the unfolding events on Earth, particularly the impending changes that ripple across our planet.

In this realm, the veil of forgetfulness thins, allowing for a more efficient gathering of memories and a heightened ability to recall intricate details of our entire experience. The Gathering offers a profound opportunity to glimpse the interplay between various cosmic intelligences, as beings from diverse corners of the physical cosmos converge in this mesmerizing space.

As you venture through these Focus levels, your consciousness transcends the boundaries of our earthly domain, immersing you in a remarkable exchange with beings from distant stars. The Gathering becomes a stage for interstellar connection, where knowledge flows freely, and insights from far-flung realms intertwine with the unfolding narrative of our earthly journey. Embrace this opportunity to explore the wonder of cosmic communication and the vastness of the universe that awaits beyond our physical horizons.

FOCUS 42
I-THERE

Focus 43—the enigmatic realm of I-There—invites us to delve into the intricacies of our existence beyond the confines of our physical self. Let's take a moment to understand this intriguing concept.

Monroe often referred to the I-There and the I-Here to distinguish between his physical being and his spiritual or energetic self. The "I" represents our self-identity, encompassing our ego, consciousness, and individuality. I-There symbolizes our spiritual essence in the vastness of the Absolute or energetic realm, while I-Here represents our earthly existence in this physical body on Earth.

In this extraordinary state of consciousness, you will:

Explore the larger I-There Cluster, unearthing new aspects of yourself, expanding your memory, and integrating the multidimensional self into your daily experiences.

Journey through inter-dimensional frontiers, bridging the parallels between outer space and inner consciousness.

Know Yourself as an Even Greater Being, gaining deeper insights into your role and place within the vast universe.

Explore life and consciousness beyond the Earth/Human realm, connecting with galactic and intergalactic realms.

Travel through the solar system and familiarize yourself with the consciousness of each planet, retrieving memories and making contact with higher intelligence and inner guidance.

Discover your intricate relationship with other life forms, embracing a broader understanding of existence.

Bring back patterns, perceptions, and visions that empower humanity and all life on Earth to embrace life-affirming futures more easily.

Explore the consciousness portal known as the Stargate of the Galactic Core, unveiling a "Different Overview" through awakening past and future memories associated with distant energy systems.

Reclaim, remember, and integrate various aspects of yourself, unraveling the mysteries of your being.

Focus 43 invites you to embrace the grand tapestry of existence, connecting with the vastness of the cosmos and unlocking the secrets of the universe within. As you venture into this realm, you'll discover the limitless potential of your consciousness and the boundless possibilities of your journey through the cosmos.

FOCUS 49
THE CLUSTER COUNCIL

At Focus 49, you reach the pinnacle of exploration, immersing yourself in what Monroe aptly describes as the "Infinite Sea of Bonded I-There Clusters." Here, you gain access to the profound wisdom of the

"Cluster Council," a higher order of guidance and enlightenment.

In this exalted state of consciousness, the boundaries between individual I-There Clusters dissolve, and a grand tapestry of interconnectedness emerges. It's as if you are part of an expansive ocean, where each drop of water represents a unique I-There Cluster, and together, they form a unified whole.

Within this boundless expanse, you have the privilege to commune with the Cluster Council—a council of enlightened beings who hold unfathomable wisdom and insight. Their guidance transcends the limitations of individual perspectives, offering a holistic understanding of existence and profound insights into the cosmic tapestry.

As you navigate through the Infinite Sea, you'll experience a profound sense of unity and interconnectedness with all beings in the universe. The wisdom imparted by the Cluster Council transcends words, and you'll find yourself immersed in a deep knowing that surpasses human comprehension.

At Focus 49, you become a part of a greater cosmic symphony, harmonizing with the collective consciousness of the bonded I-There Clusters. The guidance received from the Cluster Council empowers you to embrace your true purpose and navigate the complexities of existence with newfound clarity and grace.

As you journey through the Infinite Sea of Bonded I-There Clusters and connect with the Cluster Council, you'll realize that you are an integral thread woven into the fabric of the universe—a timeless soul on an eternal quest for growth, understanding, and enlightenment. Embrace the boundless wisdom and embrace your place in the infinite dance of existence.

How to Listen

To make the most of your Hemi-Sync® experience, follow these easy steps to prepare yourself for a transformative journey:

Find a Comfortable Space: Choose a quiet and distraction-free environment where you can relax for about an hour. Sitting or lying down is best for the exercises.

Embrace Distractions: If external noises occur during the audios, don't view them as hindrances. Instead, use them as cues to deepen your inner experience. For example, if a dog barks, see it as a sign that you're delving further into your inner self.

Prepare Your Mind and Body: Allow at least an hour after eating before beginning the Hemi-Sync® exercises. Avoid alcohol, drugs, or excessive caffeine, as they can hinder your ability to reach the desired state and reduce effectiveness.

Relax and Unwind: Take a few moments to calm your mind and put any worries aside. Use the restroom before each session, even if you think you don't need to, to prevent distractions.

Get Comfortable: Remove any constricting clothing, shoes, and eyeglasses, and do some gentle stretching. During the audio, find a comfortable position, either lying down or sitting with head support.

Move Freely: Feel free to alternate between positions during the session if needed to stay comfortable and relaxed. If you experience an itch, scratch it, and gently return to your relaxation state.

Be Prepared for Sensations: As you begin the session, your metabolic rate may change, leading to sensations of coolness, warmth, motion, or pressure. Keep a loose blanket nearby to adjust your comfort level accordingly.

By following these guidelines, you'll create an optimal space for your Hemi-Sync® journey. Remember that each experience is unique, and there is no right or wrong way to explore your consciousness. Embrace the process with an open heart and mind; allow yourself to fully immerse in the transformative power of Hemi-Sync®. Enjoy the exploration of your inner world and the potential for growth and self-discovery that lies ahead.

JOURNAL

To enhance your Hemi-Sync® journey, consider keeping a notepad handy to record the specifics of your experiences. Note down the date and time of each session, your body posture, any medications or unusual foods you've consumed, your mood and attitude, energy levels, and even the moon phase. Any other unusual circumstances or observations can also be recorded.

Having a journal dedicated to your gateway experiences can be beneficial. You can use it to delve deeper into your reflections and insights, allowing you to track your progress over time. To access a dedicated journal based on the seven waves, simply search for the other book in this series written by

Desiree M. Palmer on Amazon.com. This journal has been thoughtfully designed to help you make the most of your gateway experience and further enrich your personal growth journey.

EQUIPMENT

Audio Device: If you decide to purchase the audios from the Monroe Institute, you'll have the choice of downloading them directly to your computer or buying CDs. It's essential to have an audio playing device compatible with your chosen format. Avoid playing the audios directly from your computer, as you'll want to be in a relaxed state, either seated or lying down. To ensure convenience and portability, consider transferring the audios to a portable device like an iPod. Organize them in the correct order by numbering each audio according to its sequence in the program.

Headphones: Hemi-Sync® audios rely on separate frequencies for the left and right ears to be effective. For optimal results, use headphones that allow you to hear the audio in each ear independently. Wireless earbuds can be a great option to avoid being encumbered by cords during your experience. Noise-canceling headphones can also enhance your immersion, allowing you to fully immerse yourself in the audio without external distractions.

By setting up your audio system properly, you can create an ideal environment to delve into the transformative world of Hemi-Sync®, where you can explore new realms of consciousness and expand your personal growth journey.

VOLUME RECOMMENDATIONS

When embarking on your Hemi-Sync® journey, it's crucial to set the audio volume at a level where you can just hear it. Trust that your senses will become more heightened and attuned as you listen to the tape. Resist the temptation to turn up the volume, as doing so may lead to surprising vocal instructions during certain parts of the exercise. Avoid adjusting your headphones while the session is in progress, as the volume changes in the Hemi-Sync® frequencies are intentionally engineered.

Remember, increasing the volume won't enhance the effectiveness of the FFR (Frequency Following Response) or the disguised sound patterns. In fact, it may even diminish the benefits of the exercise. To create an optimal environment for your experience, consider using noise-canceling earphones, which can help you fully immerse yourself in the Hemi-Sync® frequencies without external disturbances, allowing you to explore new dimensions of consciousness and unlock the potential for personal growth and transformation.

WHAT YOU HEAR, WHAT TO EXPECT

The heart of the audio system is the soothing sound of ocean surf—a natural representation of energetic waves in action. By listening to this tranquil sound, you will develop the ability to sense, tune, and regulate your own vibrational energy as it flows within you. It's crucial to grasp that this process is about mastering the skill of energy regulation. As a result, you'll be empowered to harmonize with your environment in profound and diverse ways, unlike ever before.

Instead of seeking to control others and your surroundings, this journey will lead you to connect with them on a deeper level. Letting go of the need for control is a pivotal aspect of this process, which aligns with the teachings of various religions. Embracing the ability to surrender control and allow the divine to work through us is essential for true transformation and enlightenment on this extraordinary expedition of self-discovery and growth.

PRECAUTIONS AND WARNINGS

This training system is designed for self-exploration and personal growth. However, it's crucial to recognize that it is not psychotherapy, philosophy, religious doctrine, or medical treatment. Rather, it offers a method of acquiring knowledge and applying it to enhance your life. Please be aware that you are solely responsible for how you use this program.

It's essential to remember that the Hemi-Sync® audio course is not a substitute for any medical treatments or diagnoses. Therefore, if you have any medical concerns or conditions, consult with your healthcare provider before using the audios.

For your safety, refrain from listening to Hemi-Sync® audios while driving or operating heavy machinery. Additionally, avoid using these audios in conjunction with other devices that could influence brainwave activities, as this may disrupt the intended effects.

If you have a history of seizures, auditory disorders, or severe mental conditions, it is important to consult your doctor before using Hemi-Sync® audios.

Always pay attention to your body and mind while using the audios. If you experience any unusual physical or mental sensations that make you uncomfortable, stop using the program immediately.

Now, let's delve into the audio course itself, so you can embark on this transformative journey of exploration and growth.

Wave I: Discovery

Welcome to Wave I, the foundational step in The Gateway Experience. This phase is all about self-discovery and unlocking the portal to your ideal state of being. Think of the audios as training wheels on a bicycle. They are crucial in the beginning, just like you need them to learn to ride a bike. However, relying on them forever can hinder your progress. The goal is to eventually be able to conduct the exercises on your own, without the audios.

Through the Discovery album, you'll familiarize yourself with the audios, the method, and the process. This isn't just about learning concepts through reading; it's about gaining firsthand experience through practice. Engaging in these activities will expand your knowledge beyond what you already know or have read about.

While the book helps you understand how things work and eliminate doubts, the true transformation comes from engaging with the audios. Listening and learning with your sensing, or right brain, is a whole different experience compared to merely reading and learning with your left brain, the logical part of yourself.

As you journey through Wave I, take your time to understand and grasp each concept fully. The goal is to be able to do the exercises on your own, in any situation, without relying on the audios. Achieving this level of mastery is essential before moving on to the next wave.

Depending on your prior experience with altered states of consciousness and meditation, it may take time to recreate and fully embrace these foundational concepts. Some learners may feel challenged when their minds resist calming down. Remember that your mind's instinct is to protect itself, and accessing the right brain requires bypassing the left brain's filter. Be patient and thank your left brain for its vigilance while reassuring it that you are safe.

During the exercises, you may experience moments of disengagement or "Click Out." This is different from nodding off; you remain actively engaged in the exercise even if you click out. While time may feel elusive during this state, your experiences are still imprinted in your brain. It's not uncommon to click out during moments of solo exploration.

Your curiosity and outcomes will flourish as you let go of attachment to specific results. The paradox of The Gateway Experience lies in how your discovery is influenced by what you already know and expect.

Embrace a state of no expectations at the beginning, middle, and end of each exercise to foster continuous growth.

The journey commences at Focus 10, so don't be surprised. Ensure you follow the audios in the recorded order. Focus 10 emphasizes the harmony between doing and being, where idea and action, imagination and reality, self and universe synchronize. This state allows for "flow entry" when the serious and fun aspects of self-discovery intertwine, and effort and fun are no longer opposing forces. Achieving Focus 10 marks a significant step in your transformative journey.

As you progress through Wave I, keep an open mind and let the exploration lead you to new revelations. Each step is an invitation to unlock hidden potential and unleash your inner self. Enjoy the process and embrace the growth that awaits you on this extraordinary expedition.

Discovery #1: Orientation

As you progress through each audio in the Discovery Wave, you'll notice a gradual build-up of skills, activities, and experiences. The Gateway Experience is a cumulative journey, with each audio and wave incorporating elements from those that came before it. As you become more familiar with the earlier audios, you'll find it easier to master the subsequent ones.

During your first session with each audio, follow the instructions precisely. Afterward, you can listen again and make adjustments that feel more aligned with your personal journey. Allow your heart to guide you and be open to being carried forward by the current of your unique experiences. Remember that no two people will have the same journey, as individual filters shape our perceptions.

If you're completing this training with others, don't be discouraged if your experiences differ from theirs. Each person's path is distinct, and that's perfectly normal. To gain a deeper understanding, some find it helpful to listen to the audios actively at first, without trying to have any specific experience, and not in a state of meditation. This approach can prevent the mind from anticipating what might come next during the practice.

It's essential to be loose and playful with the audios, trying different methods to find what works best for you. There's no right or wrong way to experience The

Gateway. As you listen to the audios, you'll grow stronger, more focused, and better able to comprehend the insights you receive. Revisiting the basic audios can also reinforce your understanding.

Keep in mind that for most people, these experiences may feel like imagination. Don't dismiss them as merely creations of your mind. All imagination is inspired by our connection to our higher self. To discern the difference, pay attention to the ideas that come to you spontaneously. If they "pop" into your mind without conscious effort, it's likely that they are inspired by a higher source rather than being a product of your deliberate thought.

One significant aspect of the Discovery audios is the creation of various devices in your mind scape. Trust what spontaneously emerges in your mind and follow those ideas immediately. These devices will play a crucial role throughout the entire process, so take note of them and keep them in mind. Here's a brief overview of some of these devices to help you navigate this exciting journey.

ENERGY CONVERSION BOX (ECB)

In your mind scape, you will create a "box" that serves as a part of your personal space. This box will be used to hold your worries and concerns during the exercises, allowing you to free yourself from distractions. Remember, this is not a physical box but a thought form, a product of your imagination.

Customize your External Container Box (ECB) to make it uniquely yours. It should help you detach from anything that hinders your progress towards your goals. The box can be simple or intricate, traditional, or high-tech, and made of physical or non-physical materials. It could be anything from a rustic wooden chest to an intricately designed marble container, from a vacuum cleaner to a nuclear particle collector, or even from a lead-lined box to a luminous sphere – there are no limitations on its appearance. The essential aspect is that it serves as a container with a way to open it and place other thought forms inside.

Throughout your journey, you may notice changes in the size, shape, or color of your box. Embrace these changes, as they symbolize your personal growth and transformation as you progress through the process.

During the exercises, you will fill your ECB with tangible representations of your worries or distractions. Once you have placed them inside, close the box and set it aside for the duration of the audio session. This symbolic act helps you mentally set aside your concerns, freeing your mind to explore and fully engage with the transformative experience.

RESONANT FREQUENCY TUNING

When the time comes to fill your box, you will visualize physical symbols that represent your distractions. To prepare for this, it's helpful to brainstorm and create a list of everything that might distract you during the exercises. Make these symbols personal to you, rather than general, so they hold specific meaning. For example, you could imagine a wallet to represent financial worries, a photo or doll to symbolize someone on your mind, or any other item that resonates with you.

By creating physical representations of your distractions, you ensure that whatever you place inside the box stays contained during the exercise. You can also create symbols for restrictive words like "can't," "shouldn't," "must," and "never." Experiment and find what works best for you, and don't hesitate to represent past, present, and future concerns.

Allow your representations to change and transform as needed, adapting to your evolving needs. Remember not to obsess over any aspect of the exercise, including the box creation and filling. Approach the journey with ease and without judgment. Trust that your experience will unfold perfectly for you.

If at any point during the session you feel the need to return to your box and add more distractions, you are free to do so. The box is a tool for your self-discovery, and you have the liberty to interact with it as you see fit. Embrace the process with an open heart and an open mind, and let your journey be a unique and transformative experience.

AFFIRMATION

During your Hemi-Sync® journey, you will receive the Gateway Affirmation, which serves various purposes, such as:

Focusing Your Attention: The affirmation helps you concentrate on the specific goal you wish to achieve during each exercise, keeping your mind centered and aligned with your intentions.

Expanding Consciousness: By focusing on the affirmation, you become more aware of your consciousness expanding and opening up to new experiences and insights.

Collaboration with Energy: The affirmation allows you to respond to and cooperate with different types of energy and energy systems you may encounter during your exploration.

Embracing Positive Influences: The Gateway Affirmation helps you maintain a state of calmness and openness, making you receptive to positive influences and insights during your journey.

By incorporating the Gateway Affirmation into your experience, you can enhance your self-discovery and personal growth, creating a deeper connection with your inner self and the vast potentials of consciousness.

HEMI-SYNC GATEWAY PROCESS AFFIRMATION:

I am more than my physical body.

Because I am more than physical matter, I can perceive that which is greater than the physical world.

Therefore, I deeply desire to expand, experience, know, use, control, and understand how to use such greater energies and energy systems as are beneficial and constructive to me and to those who follow me.

I deeply desire the help, cooperation, assistance, and understanding of those individuals whose wisdom, development, and experience are equal or greater than my own.

I ask for their guidance, and their protection from any outside influence or source that might provide me with less than my stated desires.

RESONANT TUNING

Robert Monroe coined the term "resonant tuning" to describe what is commonly known as nonphysical energy or second-state energy. This vital energy flows along the lines of energy within our bodies, following the principle that our bodies, like the universe, operate bilaterally with positive and negative poles, akin to batteries.

One widely used technique to replenish and revitalize this energy is through breathing exercises. These exercises serve as a universal method to recharge our "battery" and promote a harmonious flow of energy. By moving this energy through its natural channels, such as energy meridians and chakras, we can release knots and blockages, bringing about a realignment and balance in our body's chemistry. These practices contribute to our overall well-being and support our journey of self-exploration and personal development.

Side Note on our energy systems.

The understanding of our energy systems is no longer limited to theoretical or philosophical concepts. Recent research conducted by experts at Seoul National University has confirmed the existence of meridians, now referred to as the "primo-vascular system." This system has been recognized as an integral part of the cardiovascular system and is believed to be the physical basis of the Acupuncture Meridian System.

Furthermore, the primo-vascular system is thought to play a role in the transmission of energy and information through biophotons, which are electromagnetic waves of light, and DNA. This discovery lends support to the traditional Chinese Medicine's belief in meridians, which are not merely superficial but are concrete ducts that extend deep within the body.

Additional investigations using imaging techniques and CT scans have further validated the ancient map of acupuncture points used by Chinese energy practitioners. Through contrast CT imaging, researchers found distinct microvascular structures concentrated at acupuncture points, highlighting their unique and significant role in the body's energy system.

These scientific findings provide tangible evidence for the existence and significance of our energy systems, and they offer a bridge between ancient healing practices and modern scientific understanding. The exploration of these energy systems holds great promise for our self-discovery and pursuit of holistic well-being.

(Back to Resonant Tuning.)

The Resonant Tuning breathing technique serves as a powerful method to recharge and rejuvenate your entire body while reducing internal chatter. It is not only beneficial for preparing you for the Gateway exercises but can also be used for meditation and to cultivate a sense of calm.

During the practice of Resonant Tuning, you may experience sudden jerks or twitches, or even sensations akin to a headache. Although these occurrences may seem unusual, it's important to confront them without resistance. Allowing the experience to flow through you will enable you to progress and move forward.

Follow the pacing on the audio during the breathing exercises, adjusting the rhythm according to your comfort level. Continue vocalizing the "aaah," "oooh," and "uuum" sounds, using your physical vocal cords to make the sounds. As the process unfolds, you may notice responses in your body as it aligns with resonant energy.

Visualize an abundant and vibrant energy enveloping you as you take a deep breath, allowing this vital force to spread throughout your entire body, including your head. As you hold your breath, let the energy gently swirl within your head, maintaining its flow. When exhaling, do so slowly through your lips, as though gently extinguishing a candle. This helps release any stagnant energy from your body through the soles of your feet.

To deepen your awareness of your control over autonomic behavior, synchronize your eye movement with your breathing patterns. Open your eyes as you inhale and close them as you exhale. This practice allows you to realize that you can consciously influence automatic processes like blinking and breathing, ultimately gaining more control over your habitual behaviors and reflexes.

Inhale = OPEN EYE

Exhale = CLOSE EYES

The Resonant Tuning technique offers an empowering means of connecting with your energy, enabling you to harmonize with your inner self and experience profound shifts in your consciousness. Through consistent practice, you can cultivate a greater sense of self-awareness and open new pathways to personal growth and transformation.

RETURN TO FULL WAKING CONSCIOUSNESS

At the conclusion of each tape exercise, a strong audio signal (C-1) will play, signaling the transition to full waking consciousness. When you hear this signal, simply open your eyes and breathe normally to return to your physical awareness. Alternatively, you can activate your entire body by moving the fingers on your right hand, which will also bring you back to waking physical consciousness.

It's crucial to resist the temptation of removing your headphones too quickly. Allow yourself to continue listening to the signal until it is completely turned off. This process ensures a complete disengagement from the exercise's stimulation. The more you challenge yourself to fully recover from one exercise, the better prepared you'll be to tackle the next one.

By giving yourself the time to integrate the experience and gradually return to the present moment, you enhance the effectiveness of the exercises and facilitate a smoother transition between altered states of consciousness and waking reality. Embrace the journey with patience and mindfulness, trusting that each step of the process contributes to your personal growth and exploration of the mind's potential.

Discovery #2: Introduction to Focus 10

In Focus 10, your mind remains awake and alert, while your body enters a state of peaceful and deep slumber. This state is also known as the 10-State or C-10, and throughout the training, these terms will be used interchangeably to refer to the same state of consciousness.

To achieve Focus 10, you will begin with Focus 3 and gradually relax your facial muscles, followed by releasing your attention. By doing so, your brain will recognize and understand this state, allowing relaxation to spread throughout your entire body and mind. Take your time and go through the steps slowly, focusing on each body part and then completely relaxing it as you proceed.

During this process, you may be asked to visualize your foot "with your closed eyes." This action helps you attain a sense of detachment from the situation, facilitating a deeper level of relaxation.

As you count from four to ten, you will systematically release tension from each part of your physical self. Since your mind remains awake while your body sleeps, you may become more aware of various physical aspects such as twitching, tingling, changes in temperature, and other sensations. You might also notice your heartbeat and the sound of blood flowing through your ears as you breathe. Additionally, subtle odors or sounds may become more perceptible. When these sensations arise, you can acknowledge and place them in your ECB (Energy Conversion Box).

The journey through Focus 10 is a significant step in the Gateway Experience, allowing you to access altered states of consciousness while retaining awareness and control. Embrace the process with patience and openness, and let your experiences guide you on this transformative exploration of your inner self.

HEALTH AFFIRMATION

After your session, you will find that your body has returned to a state of perfect balance, allowing you to overcome anything that might hinder your mental, spiritual, and physical well-being. In this balanced state, your body can enter a state of self-healing, where energy is used to correct imbalances and clear blockages, enabling the natural healing process to take place.

Think of self-healing as our body's innate ability. Consider the analogy of pregnancy to understand this better. When a single fertilized cell begins the process of forming a human being inside a woman's womb, it does not need external programming or initiation from a doctor. That single cell contains all the information required to create an entire functioning human being. It knows when to form an arm, grow a heart, and develop every part of the body. This intricate information is stored within the hologram of the egg and sperm cell.

Similarly, our bodies contain all the information needed in our original hologram to maintain and

230

improve our functioning throughout life. However, as we go through life, we encounter various traumas, energetic, mental, and physical, that can disrupt our natural balance and functioning. These disruptions create energetic trauma, and if not released, they can lead to physical traumas or imbalances. For instance, a tumor may develop due to inconsistent and misaligned energy in a cell, causing it to replicate uncontrollably.

During the Gateway Experience, when you hear and are guided through a health affirmation, it is essential to remain open and allow yourself to release energetic blocks and trauma, even if you haven't consciously identified what they are. The power of the affirmation and the energy work during the session can help facilitate the release and clearing of blockages, contributing to your overall well-being and allowing your body to move towards a state of self-healing and harmony. Trust in the process and embrace the transformative potential that lies within.

Discovery #3: Advanced Focus 10

In Advanced Focus 10, you will delve deeper into the use of various devices that will enhance your experience and training. These devices are tools to help you navigate and explore different states of consciousness and expand your understanding of your inner self and the universe. Let's explore some of these advanced devices:

Energy Conversion Box (ECB): As mentioned earlier, the ECB serves as a container for your worries and distractions during the exercises. It allows you to release these concerns temporarily, freeing your mind to explore and connect with higher states of consciousness.

The Mental Screen: This is a visualization technique that allows you to create and interact with vivid mental images on an imaginary screen in your mind. You can use the mental screen to visualize different scenarios, symbols, or concepts, aiding in self-discovery and problem-solving.

The Mental Gymnasium: This device enables you to exercise and develop your mental faculties, enhancing your focus, intuition, and creativity. Just like physical exercise strengthens your body, mental exercises in the mental gymnasium strengthen your mind and consciousness.

The Mental Laboratory: The mental laboratory is a space in your mind where you can experiment with different thoughts, ideas, and concepts. It allows you to explore various perspectives and gain insights into your beliefs and understanding of reality.

The Energy Barometer: This device helps you gauge your energy levels and the intensity of your experiences during the exercises. It allows you to become more aware of shifts in your energy and consciousness, helping you fine-tune your practice.

The Resonance Recorder: This device allows you to track and analyze your experiences and progress over time. You can use it to keep a record of your journey, insights, and discoveries, helping you identify patterns and areas of growth.

The Focus Point: This is a mental anchor that you can use to maintain your focus and awareness during the exercises. It could be a symbol, word, or image that helps you stay centered and present throughout the journey.

As you become more familiar with these advanced devices, you will find that they enhance your ability to explore and interact with different levels of consciousness. They are tools to assist you in your self-exploration and personal development, allowing you to go deeper into your inner world and discover profound insights about yourself and the nature of reality. Remember, the more you practice and engage with these devices, the more profound and transformative your experiences can become. Embrace the journey with an open heart and an adventurous spirit, and you will uncover the limitless potential that lies within you.

Nonetheless, we start with the Resonate Energy Balloon.

RESONANT ENERGY BALLOON (REBAL)

By utilizing Resonant Tuning and the REBAL technique, you can harness the recharged and revitalized energy from the previous exercises to create a moving field of energy around yourself. This field is known as REBAL, which stands for "Recharge, Energize, Balance, and Align." To begin, visualize this energy field as a ball of vibrant energy surrounding your body.

Start the process by allowing the energy to flow out from the top or crown of your head like a fountain. Feel it move gently down and around you in a natural spiral pattern. This flow of energy is essential for harmonizing and balancing your energy system. As you become more proficient, you can adapt the flow pattern to a spiral, enabling you to draw energy in from your surroundings and coil it back within yourself.

This technique aligns with your energy system's natural rhythm and allows you to draw in and utilize positive energy from the universe. Through this practice, you can experience a deeper connection with your own energetic being and the larger cosmic energies that surround you.

It is worth noting that during energy healing sessions, practitioners often observe similar patterns and utilize various methods to restore balance and harmony in a person's energy field. By incorporating the REBAL technique, you can become more in tune with your energy system and promote a harmonious flow of energy throughout your body, enhancing your overall well-being and self-awareness. With continued practice, you may discover profound insights into your energy dynamics and foster a sense of balance and alignment within yourself.

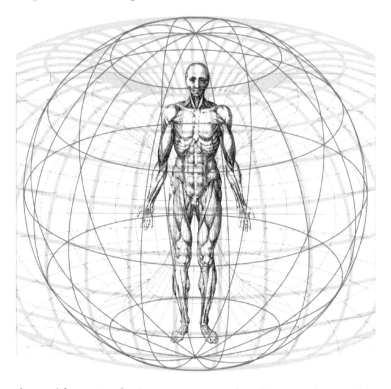

As a side note, during my energy healing sessions with clients, I often observe this phenomenon known as the REBAL (Resonant Energy Balloon) described in this material. In this process, I can perceive holes, colors, or distortions within their energy field. By collaborating with the person's own "higher realm" team, we work together to repair and restore their energy flow to its natural state.

One crucial lesson I've learned is the significance of not imposing expectations or my own biases onto what I perceive. An enlightening example involves a client who had hundreds of holes in the back of their energy pattern. As I focused on repairing these areas, they shared with me that they had recently left a job at a jail. During their time there, they always felt as if prisoners were directing negative energy towards their back, which affected their well-being. If I had allowed doubts or judgment to cloud my perception, I might have misinterpreted the root cause of their discomfort and hindered their healing process.

It is evident that when a person's energy is flowing smoothly and remains balanced, their body can work more efficiently on self-healing. However, when energetic imbalances occur, the body must navigate around these roadblocks, impacting overall well-being.

By maintaining an open, non-judgmental approach to energy healing, I enable the person's energy system to be restored to its natural and harmonious flow. This empowers their innate healing abilities, allowing them to embark on a journey of holistic healing and personal growth.

Your REBAL is an incredibly powerful tool for cultivating a heightened energy state within and around you. During these sessions, your energetic state will attract and resonate with items and energies that align with its magnetism, much like a magnet attracts items that resonate with its own field. It also serves as a protective shield, safeguarding you from harmful energies. As you spend more time developing your connection to your REBAL, you will find it easier to maintain higher energy levels in your daily life. You can detect its presence through your feelings and treat it like a charged battery, carrying it with you wherever you go. In time, you will become more aware of your energy balloon and will be able to access and utilize it at will.

With practice, you can learn to engage your REBAL, activating or expanding it while in either C-1 or Focus 10. All it takes is a single resonant energy breath to initiate this process. Inhale life-giving energy and visualize a brilliant, moving circle surrounding you as you hold this image. As you exhale, allow the energy to flow down, around, and over your entire being. Your REBAL will be automatically reabsorbed into your energy field after use.

Your natural energy flow follows the pattern of moving out through your head, around your body, and then reentering through your feet. This is why the practice of "grounding" or connecting with the earth, such as by being barefoot in nature, is so beneficial. The natural frequency of the earth is directly absorbed into your energy field, enhancing your energetic balance and vitality.

It is essential to understand that your energy field has an infinite amount of energy available to it. You cannot exhaust or deplete this energy reserve, and it will always be accessible to support your well-being and personal growth.

Experiment.

Explore the capabilities of your REBAL by testing it in various situations. For instance, try being in front of a group of people to observe if the resonance elicits a response from those who are attuned to your frequency. Notice if it captures their attention in a manner similar to how striking a tuning fork activates others who are in harmony with it. Another experiment you can conduct is wrapping your REBAL around the outside of your car while driving. Observe whether this adjustment leads to smoother traffic patterns or makes it easier to find parking spaces.

When you activate your REBAL, you amplify your own energy, creating a high-energy state both within and around yourself. Operating on the principle of resonance and aligned with the Gateway Affirmation, your REBAL acts as a filter, permitting only energy that matches or surpasses your own to enter your energy field. Consequently, it acts as a protective shield against unwanted energy influences. Just like a magnet attracts higher energy forms, your REBAL attracts and aligns with elevated energy states. As you develop your REBAL, your physical body becomes capable of holding increasing amounts of energy, eventually allowing you to use Focus 10 as an energy launch pad, propelling you into other states of consciousness.

A high-energy state involves heightened awareness and encompasses perception mechanisms beyond those commonly utilized in waking consciousness. This expanded awareness allows you to access a broader range of perceptions, which can be harnessed for problem-solving, creativity, seeking guidance, or simply experiencing a more acute interaction with your inner and outer realities.

It's essential to note that a high-energy state is distinct from hyperactivity or having an excess of energy in the body. It is not "better" than any other level of awareness but represents a personal expansion and integration of consciousness that leads to a more fulfilling life.

Your REBAL may spontaneously transform into different energy flow forms depending on the situation. For example, it might adopt a delicate membrane rather than a force field or emanate brilliance akin to an amplified aura. Our perception of our REBAL is often influenced by our current reality, much like a fish in the ocean unaware of the water it swims in. While you may not always sense your REBAL directly, experimenting with different ways of sensing it can be beneficial. Visualization, feelings, and muscle sensations are just a few possibilities for detecting your REBAL. Creating a biofeedback loop by understanding what it "feels" like to connect with your REBAL will allow you to tap into it whenever needed. Paying attention to this sensation helps train yourself, as discussed in the CIA document.

Discovery #4: Release and Recharge

Release and Recharge is a daily practice that can be performed with or without the audios, designed to recognize, release, and transform self-imposed emotions, particularly fear. While learned fear can serve as a useful warning signal, once recognized, you no longer need to hold onto that sensation or emotion.

When you enter Focus 10, you can gently explore and release anxieties, barriers, limits, or any other impediments to your personal growth. Additionally, you can replenish blocked energy with the pure energy that existed before your progress was hindered.

In this exercise, the term "fear" represents the principal emotional charge associated with a specific self-imposed barrier or limit, while "feeling" denotes the accompanying emotional charges linked with that block or limit. To gain a clearer understanding of the fear you wish to release, try to recall a specific point in your past when you experienced it. By revisiting those emotions and physical experiences, you create a stronger connection to the fear you aim to release. Just as in my earlier book, Energy Evolution, where I discussed a method for releasing traumas in genetic history, specificity about the inciting incident is critical to success.

Opening your ECB, you will sense the first wave of fear you encounter. Bring that fear out of the box and imagine it moving away from you like a bubble rising to the surface of a pool. Once the fear has passed, you can now perceive the emotion that the fear obscured. Let that emotion bubble away and release what you no longer need. Allow yourself to perceive the clean energy of the memory that had been obscured and covered up by fear and emotion. Bring that fresh, clean energy back into your body. Even if nothing comes to mind or it feels like nothing is happening, accept that the process may be functioning on deeper levels of consciousness.

Be aware of your ego's inclination to maintain its hold on your fears. Even if you believe you have already dealt with a fear, it is beneficial to continue the exercise. After letting go of your fears, you can reconnect with the delightful sensations you experienced as a youngster when sharing your experiences with others. You'll rediscover the joy of communicating with others and sharing yourself.

Once you feel comfortable with the practice as stated, you can experiment with purposefully depositing and retrieving symbols from your box to symbolize anything interfering with your ability to handle fear and emotion. For example, if an unconscious fear of having an out-of-body experience hinders your progression, place a symbol for this fear in the box and follow the instructions to release it.

Keep in mind that this is not a quick fix or a one-time remedy. Many self-imposed constraints have multiple layers and may require repeated efforts to release. This exercise is truly one of the most beneficial in the entire Gateway training. Phobias can range from beliefs you once held to those passed down through your DNA from your ancestors.

To overcome your restrictions, invest significant time, both in and out of session, in building a comprehensive list of anxieties and accompanying feelings. Take the necessary time to let these go before moving forward. If you encounter new phobias during the training, take note of them and return to this practice to release them. Many people use Release and Recharge daily to rid themselves of present tensions or disappointments. Reflecting and finding the gift in fear is crucial, as it allows you to loosen your hold on the negative aspect of fear and begin to transmute it into love.

This moderate energy conversion practice cleanses, balances, and revitalizes your entire system, leading to improved overall health.

Discovery #5: Exploration Sleep

Once you have become completely comfortable with audios 1 through 4, you should proceed with this tape.

In this exercise, we will utilize the concept that sleep serves as a natural gateway into other states of reality and other energy systems, facilitating out-of-body exploration. To enter these nonphysical states, a nonphysical consciousness capable of moving "out" of the physical body is required. Therefore, for the duration of this activity, you should be in a sleeping position.

The word "ecstasy" originally meant "to be outside of oneself," but its modern usage has evolved to refer to the sensation of being transported, experiencing incredible freedom and rapture as we return to our most natural state of being. During sleep, achieving these states of being "outside of oneself" and euphoria is simple and effortless, even though they are seldom remembered later. Through this exercise, we will bring into C-1 a common and natural process that occurs during sleep, bridging the gap between different levels of consciousness.

By recognizing that sleep offers a gateway to different states of being, we can use this knowledge to explore nonphysical realms and consciousness. As you follow the instructions on this tape, your mind will remain awake and alert, while your body is relaxed and comfortable in a sleeping position. This state of focused relaxation will allow you to access new levels of consciousness and explore the possibilities beyond your physical body.

Stay open to the experience and trust that your consciousness can navigate through different realms and energy systems. With practice, you will become more adept at entering these nonphysical states and accessing higher levels of awareness.

Remember, this exercise is meant to be exploratory and transformative. Embrace the concept of sleep as a natural gateway, and allow yourself to venture into new realms of consciousness with a sense of curiosity and wonder. Keep an open mind, and don't be discouraged if the results are not immediate. With time and practice, you will expand your consciousness and explore the limitless possibilities that lie beyond your physical body.

OUT-OF-BODY EXERCISES DURING SLEEP

Approach this exercise with a playful sense of curiosity and interest, free from unrealistic expectations. Allow any preconceived notions or doubts to go and simply relax. You can use an affirmation such as "I am completely free of expectations and open to any and all experiences that await me" to reinforce this mindset. Avoid questioning yourself during the exercise, as it may hinder the process. Instead, fully immerse yourself in the experience without judgment or analysis.

Keep in mind that you may perceive things in various ways, and that's perfectly normal. Don't worry about whether you are "doing it right" or if you are experiencing exactly what you are supposed to. After the exercise, you will have time to reflect on your experiences and expectations.

As you enter Focus 10, you may re-experience and remember any out-of-body experiences you have had while sleeping in the past. Imagine the feeling of relaxation and weightlessness as you float away from everything. Visualize yourself gently rolling over like a log drifting in water, effortlessly and serenely. Allow yourself to detach from the ground and float upward, embracing the sense of calm and freedom.

To conclude the exercise, counting from eleven to twenty will help you ease into a normal, natural, and restful sleep. In this sleep state, you can review the exercise again and again until you fully remember it. If you wish to work consciously with out-of-body techniques, you can practice Discovery #6: Free Flow 10 and follow the instructions provided, or revisit this exercise for further exploration.

As you progress through The Gateway Experience, you will encounter more out-of-body exercises in Freedom (Wave III) that will provide you with additional opportunities for practice and exploration. Embrace this journey with an open mind and a willingness to discover the wonders of nonphysical experience.

Discovery #6: Free Flow 10

Use this tape after you are completely comfortable with audios 1 through 5.

OPEN EXPLORATION

In this exercise, you have the opportunity to define and carry out your own personal mission in Focus 10, the culminating stage of the Discovery process. Before beginning, make sure you have a clear understanding of your goal and state it succinctly and straightforwardly to ensure clarity. This journey of self-exploration is designed to provide you with various tools for exploring your consciousness. Remember that different methods may be linked to specific means of perception, and your experience might heavily rely on your individual perception of kinesthetic, visual, auditory, or intuitive cues.

Keep an open mind and remain sensitive to the various energy systems available to you. Embrace the growth of your 10-State as your commitment to self-discovery deepens, opening up new avenues of exploration. Whatever you discover in Focus 10 can be revisited in Focus 10, as your energy has already located the patterns or locations you seek. After completing this exercise, you will have the opportunity to explore and clarify your feelings, energy patterns, symbols, and messages. Use specific cues, such as emotional aspects of the experience, to unlock and understand the entire journey.

Approach your investigations from various viewpoints, and if you choose to revisit a previous experience, do so with a sense of wonder and novelty. Avoid trying to recreate the exact same situation, but instead, embrace new insights and understandings that may emerge.

If you have a specific goal in mind, write it down before starting, but be open to whatever unfolds during the exercise. Avoid rigid expectations about when and how guidance should arrive, as this might hinder your ability to receive the knowledge you seek. Be receptive to various forms of perception, such as tingles, twitches, or intuitive insights. Sometimes valuable insights may come from unexpected sources.

Use repetitions of this exercise to experiment with specific tools like your affirmation box or REBAL from different angles. Each time you work with the exercise, explore it in unique ways, celebrating your individuality and the uniqueness of your experiences. While it is acceptable to revisit a previous experience, do so with an open mind and a willingness to embrace new discoveries rather than trying to recreate the past exactly as it occurred.

GUIDANCE

In Focus 10, it is essential to seek only the knowledge you genuinely desire and to take responsibility for what you learn, as it becomes integrated into your everyday life. You don't need to know the specific destination or path of guidance; instead, choose to follow the instructions provided. Setting rigid expectations about when or how guidance should arrive might hinder you from receiving the information you seek.

Feeling gratitude is a powerful acknowledgment of receiving something beyond your conscious boundaries of self-perception. Expressions of gratitude act like antennas, enhancing the flow of energy and communication. When you cultivate a sense of gratitude, it fosters cooperation and, in turn, inspires even more gratitude and positive interactions. Embracing gratitude and cooperation can greatly enrich your experiences in the Focus 10 state and beyond.

FREE FLOW METHODS OF EXPLORATION

During Focus 10, you can engage in the process of answering questions, resolving problems, and receiving messages. To do this, focus your attention on the question or problem you want to explore. Push it out from your center of consciousness, allowing it to flow out in all directions before releasing it. This can be combined with the One-Breath Technique in C-1: Inhale vital energy while thinking "ten," hold the question in your mind while thinking "hold," and then exhale while sending the question out.

The key factors for successful information reception are your genuine desire to know, the clarity of your intent, and the intensity with which you send out that desire. Be patient and open to receiving the answer in its own time and manner. Expressing gratitude is crucial as well.

In Focus 10, traditional relationships between questions and answers, problems and solutions, may change as new perspectives alter the nature of the original inquiry. Focus 10 allows for a dynamic problem-solving process where solutions can be found in unexpected ways. Sometimes the question itself may not be the actual problem, and new insights can emerge when exploring the issue from different angles.

Experiment with creative monologue techniques during Focus 10. Give your box a voice, "become" your box, or allow your box to communicate in unique ways. Humor can also be beneficial in shifting perspectives and unlocking new understandings.

Be aware that if guidance comes from a more comprehensive energy system than C-1, it may alter the way questions and problems are framed. So, you can ask broad or specific questions, depending on what feels right for you.

Finally, keep an open mind and pay attention to subtle messages or humor that may provide valuable insights during your Focus 10 exploration.

LANDSCAPING

During the Gateway Voyage and other similar experiences, some individuals may choose to landscape their inner path intentionally or unintentionally, much like how Focus 3 serves as a signpost leading to Focus 10. Each numerical count can carry significance or meaning to the individual, and these counts can vary among different people.

For example, in one instance, the count of two might represent undirected energy, and the count of three might signify the use of Hemi-Sync® technology. In another case, a person may associate the count of four with a new environment, the count of five with a turning point, the count of six with the beginning of transformation, and the count of seven with the entry into Focus 10.

The important thing to recognize is that there are no universal rules or "right" places for certain events to occur within one's consciousness. Each person's inner landscape and the meaning they attach to different counts or stages are unique to them. As you move through different states of consciousness, your perceptions and experiences may change, leading to shifts in your inner landscape design.

This flexibility and variability in individual experiences are natural and part of the personal journey through altered states of consciousness. Embrace your own experiences and interpretations without judgment, as they are a reflection of your unique consciousness and inner exploration.

EXPLORE

As you count from one to ten, you will notice a gradual deepening of your 10-State, allowing you to explore different levels of consciousness and awareness. Each time you reach a new level, you will experience a profound shift in your 10-State, providing you with new insights and experiences.

During your explorations, you can experiment with different types of energy and perceptions. For instance, you can visualize yourself standing under a waterfall and then in the warm sunlight, observing whether you can sense distinct qualities in the energy surrounding you. You may notice how the energy feels different in each setting.

You can also engage your imagination to connect with other elements of nature, such as a rock or crystal. Merge with it in your mind and sense its unique ability to pattern or structure energy. Additionally, you can envision constructing a pyramid or other geometric structure around yourself and feel the pattern of energy it generates.

Furthermore, you can use your REBAL to resonate with a tree or a flower, seeking to establish communication and potentially develop a bond with the living energy of nature.

As you delve deeper into altered states of consciousness, you might encounter nonphysical energy or energy systems. Be open to exploring and communicating with these realms, expanding your understanding and connection with the larger universe.

Remember, your imagination and intention are powerful tools for these explorations. Embrace the wonder of the experience and allow your consciousness to guide you on this fascinating journey of self-discovery and connection with the world around you.

NEED GROUNDING?

If you ever feel the need for grounding or to regain your alertness after listening to the exercises, try the following basic techniques:

Counting Backwards: Take a deep breath and slowly count backwards from one to one hundred. This simple technique can help bring you back to the present moment and restore your focus.

Drinking Water: Drink a glass of cool water immediately after completing the audio exercises. Hydrating yourself can help refresh your body and mind.

Cold Water Splash: Wash your face, neck, and wrists with ice water or take a cold shower. The cold water can invigorate your senses and awaken your awareness.

Barefoot Walking: If the weather permits, walk barefoot outdoors. Take deep breaths and allow any excess energy to flow out through your feet, connecting with the stabilizing energy of the earth.

Tree Connection: Find a tree and lean your back against it. Visualize energy flowing out of the top of your head, reaching the branches above you. Then, visualize energy flowing out of the soles of your feet, connecting with the tree's roots below. Allow the tree's grounding energy to help you regain your balance.

These techniques can be beneficial for bringing you back to a state of groundedness and alertness after your exploration in altered states of consciousness. Remember that each person's experience may vary, so find what works best for you and incorporate it into your post-exercise routine.

Wave II: Threshold

In Threshold, you will venture into new territory and experience Focus 12, a state of expanded awareness that you have not encountered before. Alongside this, you will have the opportunity to further develop and refine your Focus 10 (mind awake/body asleep) skills.

It's crucial to understand that each Wave in the Gateway Experience builds upon the foundations of the preceding Waves. Threshold directly builds upon the tools and techniques taught in Discovery, as well as the information provided in the Discovery instructions. Therefore, it is recommended to engage in Threshold exercises only after completing Discovery and gaining prior experience with those techniques.

FOCUS 12: AN OVERVIEW

Focus 12 is characterized by heightened energy levels, enabling you to explore and become more conscious of your inner resources and guidance. Techniques previously covered in Discovery can also be applied in specific Focus 12 audios, leading to entirely new experiences at these higher energy levels.

Similar to Focus 10, in Focus 12, you will discover that you don't need to know the exact path to receive guidance. Instead, trust and follow the given instructions. Not everyone will perceive nonphysical experiences in the same way as they perceive things in ordinary waking consciousness. In Focus 12, our perception of nonphysical energy can be quite different from our physical senses. Gestalt or telepathic comprehension may come into play, where we become aware of things without the need for verbal expression.

As you progress, you will learn to perceive more clearly through trust, patience, and commitment to the process of self-exploration. This clarity may occur gradually, step by step, or it could happen dramatically and suddenly, much like water breaking through a dam or a pipe.

In Threshold, be prepared for exciting new experiences as you expand your awareness and deepen your exploration of consciousness. The journey continues with new challenges and possibilities to discover.

Threshold #1: Introduction to Focus 12

In this exercise, it is essential to trust the process and allow it to unfold naturally without excessive effort. Enjoy whatever experiences arise without the need to analyze or dissect them in the moment. Trying too hard can be counterproductive; it's better to reflect on the experience after it has taken place.

Avoid getting fixated on the idea of "getting there" or achieving a specific state. Instead, let the audio guide you effortlessly into Focus 12 as you count from ten to twelve.

Stay open and receptive to change throughout your self-discovery journey. As your commitment to exploring your consciousness deepens, your ability to access and explore Focus 12 will also strengthen, providing you with new and exciting ways to expand your awareness and understanding. Embrace the process with a sense of curiosity and enjoyment as you continue your path of self-exploration.

Threshold #2: Problem Solving

In Focus 12, you can bring a problem or question to the center of your consciousness and allow it to flow out into your total awareness. Letting go of the need to force an immediate answer, you can trust that the most appropriate solution will be revealed to you in its own time and way. It's important to recognize that answers may come at a later time or from unexpected sources, and they are just as valid as immediate responses.

In this high-energy state of Focus 12, the key to receiving valuable guidance lies in your desire to know, the clarity of your question, and the intensity of your asking. Cultivating a sense of gratitude further accelerates the process of receiving insights and solutions.

As you explore Focus 12, traditional relationships between questions and answers may shift, and new perspectives can alter the nature of the original problem. Solutions are not limited to conventional alternatives, and sometimes a new question can lead to the desired answer. Simple and obvious answers should not be dismissed, as they can hold significant power and meaning.

During the exercise, answers can manifest in various forms, such as symbols, images, emotional changes, physical sensations, or sudden knowing. If no answers come immediately during the exercise, remain open and receptive as guidance can also come in different ways throughout your daily life.

If you're unsure of what to ask or what your greatest challenge is, approach the exercise from different angles, asking for the most important information you need at that moment. Be mindful of receiving guidance from higher energy systems, as limiting your questions to your current consciousness may restrict your resources.

Be creative and resourceful in your problem-solving techniques during Focus 12, experimenting with different approaches if necessary. Trust in the process, enjoy the journey, and be open to the diverse ways in which guidance may reveal itself to you.

Threshold #3: One-Month Patterning

During this exercise, we'll delve into the powerful tool of patterning, a technique that empowers you to take control of your life. You may have encountered similar techniques before, but let's explore this one in more depth.

Patterning is based on the fundamental premise that our thoughts have the power to manifest as tangible outcomes in our lives. What we consistently think and believe shapes our reality. It's not a question of whether we pattern, but rather how intensely and deliberately we choose the thoughts that occupy our minds. When we consciously make these choices while in high-energy states like Focus 12, our patterns emerge around us, reshaping our lives at a pace and intensity not possible in ordinary consciousness. Consider the possibilities of patterning as a valuable tool for self-discovery.

Think about "Phil," which represents the physical, mental, or emotional patterns you wish to see manifest in your life. Place Phil at the center of your consciousness, just like in the previous exercise, and then release it. You'll know you've successfully released the pattern when you feel a sense of ease and detachment. Be specific about your desires. For instance, do you want a new house or contentment with your current residence? Do you aim to lose ten pounds or enhance your self-confidence? In your patterning statement, use the present tense, such as "I am now receiving..." and perceive yourself as an active participant in the pattern.

The more specific and detailed your pattern, the greater the likelihood of achieving your desired outcome. Persistence is crucial – ask only for what you truly desire, and you'll almost certainly receive what you asked for. Infuse your intention with emotion and conviction to re-energize and strengthen its effectiveness. When you're done, simply ask that your pattern work for the good of your total self and let go of attachment to the outcome.

Despite the fact that a pattern set in Focus 12 can be changed or canceled in Focus 12, don't keep checking or changing it out of fear or uncertainty. You wouldn't dig up a seed to see if it's sprouting or not, would you? The beginning was simple and reasonable patterns. If you can sell your pattern for $50 and prove to yourself that it works, patterns will come more easily in the future.

For the purpose of creating a pattern, think, feel, or imagine what you want to see become a part of your daily life. Patterning functions such as problem-solving place the pattern at the center of your consciousness and either push it out or allow it to flow strongly and surely out in all directions and in all directions at the same time in all directions. Then you can let it go. It is especially important to release your pattern. If you do this, it will aid in bringing the pattern into your life. It is possible to tell whether or not you have released your pattern if you feel at ease and detached when thinking about it.

264

When applied to many aspects of one's life, the patterning process can be used to create or enhance many aspects of your life: physical identity, mental identity, emotional identity, total identity, desired location, desired activity, and desired outcome. When it comes to asking for material things, there is nothing inherently wrong with it. If you come from the school of economic thought that believes we live in a world with limited resources, it will require a shift in perspective. Assuming this is the case, please consider a completely different concept: that this is a universe of infinite abundance, and there is nothing wrong with requesting a share of that abundance.

Here are some important considerations to keep in mind when making the most of patterning:

Only use the present tense when describing the pattern, such as "I am currently receiving…" You may find yourself in the situation where you are writing in the future tense, like a sign in a supermarket window that says, "FREE SODA TOMORROW" – a tomorrow that never comes.

When you make your patterning statement, use the pronoun "I" to convey that you are an active participant in the pattern, so that it does not appear to be happening all around you and not to you.

Create a pattern exclusively for yourself.

Be very specific about what you want. Do you want a new house or do you want to be content with your current residence? Do you want to lose ten pounds, or do you want to feel more confident in yourself?

Be as specific as possible. In general, the more specific and detailed your pattern is, the better your chances of getting exactly what you want.

Make sure to ask for what you really want, because you will almost certainly receive exactly what you ask for!

Put some heart and soul into it, and you'll succeed. Your intention will be revitalized and reinforced if you are filled with strong emotion. After that, let it go. It is possible to change, reinforce, or cancel any pattern that has been established in Focus 12. However, do not keep checking on it or making changes to it because of doubts, fears, or other factors that may arise. A fisherman must leave his bait in the water for a period of time before he or she will get a bite, just as when planting a seed, you do not keep digging it up to see how it is doing.

For starters, it might be a good idea to break down large requests into smaller, more manageable chunks. Consider the following scenario: If you pattern for the first time for $10 million, at least a portion of you is likely to be skeptical that it will actually work. If you begin by patterning for $50 to $100 and demonstrate to yourself that it works, you will find that other, potentially larger patterns will come more easily.

Don't specify how your request will be fulfilled; leave it up to chance. Allow the universe, or your entire self, to decide and direct your actions.

It is always advisable to qualify your pattern by requesting that it only be used for the benefit of your entire self-interest. This exercise is intended to be completed during a one-month patterning cycle. To get around this limitation, you can request that patterns be fulfilled in other cycles: a week, a year, or even by your next birthday if you wish. Alternatively, you can simply release the pattern, allowing it to be fulfilled in due course.

Please consider this exercise as a basic introduction to the art of patterning. Then carefully consider how you would like to employ the process, incorporating the components of this exercise to make it more effective. The process of patterning may cause some of your most fundamental beliefs to be called into question, which can serve as a gateway to freedom.

Threshold #4: Color Breathing

In Focus 10, the connection between mind and body, psyche and soma, can be effectively strengthened by exploring the resonance and activation of colors within your own energy. This practice allows you to develop and control both your physical and nonphysical energies with greater ease and speed. As you master this technique, you can experiment with different colors and applications, perceiving them not only through visualization but also as sound, vibrations, or other sensations based on your unique perception.

Color perception holds significant power during this exercise. For instance, envision breathing in vibrant, sparkling energy, and as you hold it within, you'll perceive a bright green color. Upon exhaling, the calming, cleansing green energy flows down your spine, ridding your body of negative emotions, stress, and tension, leaving you feeling serene and tranquil.

To recharge your physical body and enhance abilities requiring quickness, strength, and coordination, focus on vibrant red energy. As you inhale, visualize radiant white light descending from above, filling your palms and spreading throughout your entire being. This powerful energy serves as "energy food," nourishing you on multiple levels—physical, mental, emotional, and spiritual.

For healing, restoration, and balance, direct purple energy to areas of your body that require assistance

269

while repeating the healing mantra, "heal, balance," in your mind. Remember not to apply energy directly to· the problem itself. Instead, concentrate on creating or maintaining overall bodily health. After focusing your healing energy on a specific body part, conclude the session by visualizing your body as whole and perfect, promoting sound health and not reinforcing illness.

In this continuous exchange of energies, keep in mind the possibility of gathering boundless energy from an infinite source, empowering you to use it purposefully and freely. Additionally, you can fuse your own energy with that of another person. When providing energy to someone else, respect their right to choose how to use it and avoid imposing your goals upon them. Simply offer the energy with the intention of benefiting their overall well-being, honoring their purpose, whether known to you or not.

As you progress towards Focus 12, reinforce the patterning process by affirming that the patterns you create in your mind and release into your expanded consciousness will swiftly take shape and develop in the world around you.

Stress reduction, physical strength, agility, energy nourishment, healing, and patterning are all encoded within the intricate workings of the brain. Embrace the power of "Color Breathing" to harness these energies and manifest positive changes in your life.

Threshold #5: Energy Bar Tool (EBT)

The EBT, or Energy Bar Tool, is a remarkable and versatile tool that allows you to collect and harness nonphysical energies. Throughout history and mythology, we've encountered various power sticks symbolizing the connection between human and spiritual energies, from Moses' staff transforming into a serpent to scepters representing royal authority and the Lightsabers linking Star Wars heroes to the Force. In Focus 10, you'll find or create your very personal EBT, one that resonates with your energy and holds deep significance for you.

To charge your EBT, imagine extending a dot of light into a bar and gradually turning it on and off, increasing the speed until it pulsates like a strobe. As the music quickens, dissociate from the words "on" and "off" and the rhythm of your breathing. Gradually adjust the thickness and thinness of your EBT, focusing intently on its development. You'll perceive warmth as a charged, electrically vibrating sensation that may spread throughout your body. Allow the intensity of this pulsing, vibrational energy to grow.

With Resonant Tuning, you can release excess energy, such as a sense of heat, by moving it away from your body. Many people utilize their hands as energy bar tools, constructing and sensing the pulse patterns within themselves. However, remember that you can only control your own energy and attune to external energies or harmonize with them when you're alone.

Instead of seeking control over others, establish resonance with them, as well as with animals, plants, and the Earth itself.

As you delve deeper into energy systems, your EBT will serve various purposes. In Wave III, Freedom, you'll discover its potential as a remote viewing system. It can be expanded into a vortex or tunnel through which you can explore further. You might experiment by inserting one end into your Energy Conversion Box or using it as a beacon to attract guidance and intelligence. Your EBT can have its own voice or change shape autonomously. While you may initially lead it, it might eventually lead you to new destinations. These suggestions aren't strict limitations; the forms and applications of your EBT are nearly limitless with practice.

Find a secure place to store your EBT so it's readily available whenever you need it. Keep in mind that the power of your EBT is reciprocal: as you recharge it, it will recharge you, creating a harmonious and empowering relationship between you and this extraordinary tool.

As you continue to work with your EBT, you'll find that its potential and applications are limited only by your imagination and exploration. The more you practice and develop your connection with this tool, the more you will uncover its depth and intricacy.

One significant aspect of your EBT is its ability to act as a bridge between the physical and nonphysical realms. It serves as a conduit for the flow of energy, allowing you to interact with the unseen aspects of reality. As you gain proficiency, you'll find that your

EBT can assist you in accessing higher states of consciousness, providing you with new perspectives and insights into the mysteries of existence.

Moreover, your EBT can be utilized for healing and balancing both yourself and others. By directing the pulsating energy through your body and into specific areas that require attention, you can promote well-being and restoration. Remember to maintain a sense of detached compassion when offering energy to others, allowing them to choose how they utilize it for their own benefit and growth.

As you delve deeper into the realms of consciousness and energy, you might encounter challenges or obstacles along the way. However, do not be discouraged; these hurdles are part of the learning process. Embrace them as opportunities for growth and self-discovery, and with time and practice, you'll find that your abilities with the EBT will expand and become more refined.

Keep in mind that the EBT is a tool that is intimately connected to your own consciousness. It evolves with you and responds to your intentions and emotions. Therefore, approaching this practice with an open heart and a curious mind can lead to profound experiences and revelations.

Remember that there is no rush in this journey of self-exploration and energy manipulation. Allow yourself the space to grow and adapt, celebrating every step of progress along the way. Your EBT will always be there, patiently waiting for you to return and explore the vastness of consciousness.

As you develop your relationship with your EBT, you may also find that you develop a deeper connection with yourself and the world around you. Your increased sensitivity to energy and its flow will heighten your appreciation for the interconnectedness of all things, fostering a sense of unity and harmony with the universe.

In conclusion, the EBT is a powerful and flexible tool that opens up a world of possibilities for self-discovery, healing, and spiritual growth. Embrace the journey with an open mind, and you'll find that this tool becomes an invaluable companion in your quest for understanding and mastering the energies that shape our reality.

Threshold #6: Living Body Map (LBM)

With the assistance of the LBM (Life-Force Body Map), you can delve deeper into the art of energy balancing and rejuvenation, empowering both your physical and nonphysical aspects. This exercise allows you to use energy to influence energy, acknowledging that the physical world automatically responds to these energetic shifts. By employing maps to represent your physical self, you gain a perspective and detachment that aids in the healing process.

Begin by envisioning the outline of your physical body, shimmering in sparkling white light—a representation of your pure, nonphysical energy form. The power of thought-images is as potent as visual images, creating emotional impacts and influencing energetic states, regardless of whether you are a skilled visualizer or not.

As you proceed, infuse your energy map with different colors, symbolizing the various systems of your physical body. Red represents the circulatory system, blue the nervous system, yellow the organs and glandular system, and orange the muscles and bones. This process sets the stage for using the LBM to detect any imbalances or dim areas in your energy body.

Gently place the LBM over your physical body, and if any regions appear dim or flickering, utilize bright purple healing energy from your EBT to merge and harmonize the energies. Gradually bring your entire energy body to an even, balanced, and radiant white state.

Moving through the LBM systematically, recharge each system independently with vibrant purple energy, starting with sparkling white, and progressing through the colors. Repetition and practice of this technique enhance its effectiveness over time.

Each energy tool you create and employ becomes more potent with continued use. The Gateway serves as a portal for accessing information, enabling you to explore different experiences with great impact in short periods. Practice and frequency strengthen the effectiveness of these tools.

To initiate the process, inhale vibrant, sparkling energy, and on the exhale, activate your desired energy tool—something you can discreetly do anywhere. Using focused breathwork, transition to Focus 10 or Focus 12 to achieve the desired level of awareness. With your REBAL extended, you can ask questions or create patterns in your mind.

For instance, if you encounter any negative energy, take three deep breaths, infusing soothing green energy throughout your entire being. Feel free to experiment with different energy sources—for increased alertness while driving at night, inhale the vibrant red light from taillights or stoplights, filling yourself with the strength and vitality represented by red energy.

Whenever you need a boost of energy—be it physical, emotional, mental, or spiritual—breathe deeply into your palms, drawing in nourishing energy from the source above you, like a source of energy food.

This practice of utilizing energy tools and techniques offers a transformative journey, empowering you to navigate the realms of consciousness and energy with greater insight, balance, and vitality. As you refine and integrate these practices into your life, you'll discover the boundless potential within yourself and the interconnectedness of all energy forms. Embrace this journey with an open heart, for the path of exploration and growth is limitless.

As you continue your journey of exploration and growth, you will find that the integration of energy practices into your daily life brings profound benefits. Embracing the interconnectedness of all energy forms, you'll gain a deeper understanding of the world around you and your place within it.

As you become more adept at using energy tools, you'll notice how your ability to influence and harmonize energies expands. The LBM, in particular, becomes a versatile ally in your pursuit of balance and well-being. It serves as a powerful tool for self-healing, enabling you to address physical, emotional, and mental imbalances by directing energy with intention and focus.

Remember that energy is not limited to the individual self; it can also extend beyond, allowing you to resonate and harmonize with external energies. When interacting with others, approach them with respect for their autonomy, recognizing that they have the right to choose how they engage with the energy you offer. Instead of seeking to control, practice resonance and attunement, finding harmony and connection with people, animals, plants, and the environment.

With time and practice, your energy tools will evolve and expand in their capabilities. The Gateway of consciousness will open doors to new experiences and insights, enhancing your ability to explore the vast realms of knowledge and understanding. The more you engage with these tools, the more effective and potent they become, deepening your connection to the energetic fabric of existence.

As you go about your daily life, you can subtly incorporate energy practices without drawing attention. Utilizing focused breathwork and intention, you can attune yourself to different energy states, rejuvenating and empowering yourself throughout the day. Whether you need a burst of vitality or a moment of calm, the power of energy tools is always at your disposal.

In the grand tapestry of existence, you are a creator and influencer of energies. Embrace this role with humility and wisdom, recognizing the profound impact your energetic intentions can have on yourself and the world around you.

Let your EBT, your unique Energy Body Tool, be a constant companion on this journey. Whether it's visualized as a personal talisman, a guide, or a portal, it holds the potential to lead you to new dimensions of self-awareness and transformation.

Through the fusion of ancient wisdom and modern practices, you become a steward of energy, using it for your own growth, healing, and spiritual expansion.

Embrace the art of energy manipulation with an open heart and a curious mind, for the path ahead is filled with wonders waiting to be discovered.

Remember, the key to mastery lies in persistence and dedication. Allow the energy tools to become an integral part of your life, for in doing so, you will unlock the hidden potentials within yourself and the universe.

Now, take a moment to breathe in the vibrant, sparkling energy once more, and as you exhale, carry with you the wisdom and empowerment gained from this journey. Step forward with confidence, knowing that you have the tools to shape your reality and manifest your intentions in the grand tapestry of life. Trust in the infinite abundance of the universe and the boundless potential within yourself. The journey continues, and with each step, you draw closer to the realization of your true potential as an energy alchemist.

Wave III: Freedom

Welcome to Freedom, where you will embark on a transformative journey to perceive and harness your nonphysical energy. The exercises in this wave have been thoughtfully designed to make the process of perceiving your nonphysical energy a comfortable and enjoyable experience for you. Through these exercises, you will take a significant step toward gaining conscious control over the energy system that is you and your surroundings.

Before delving into the exercises of Freedom, it's essential to note that this wave builds upon the knowledge and experiences gained in the previous waves, Discovery and Threshold. Thus, it is crucial to have completed both the Discovery and Threshold Wave exercises before venturing into Freedom. This prior experience provides a solid foundation and prepares you for the deeper explorations of this wave.

If you are new to The Gateway Experience, it is not recommended to skip ahead to Freedom without having completed the preceding waves. The exercises in this wave assume a level of familiarity with the concepts and techniques introduced in the earlier waves, and attempting them without this prior experience may result in a less effective and fulfilling experience.

By following the sequence of the waves, you will find that the techniques and exercises progressively build upon each other, leading you on a profound journey of self-discovery and personal growth. As you move through Freedom, you will have a better understanding of how to perceive and interact with your nonphysical energy in various ways, enabling you to tap into its limitless potential.

So, take the time to engage with Discovery and Threshold first, building a strong foundation and readiness for the transformative experiences that Freedom holds. Once you are well-prepared, embrace the exercises with an open mind and a willingness to explore the depths of your consciousness. The journey ahead is filled with wonder and revelation, and you have the power to unlock the extraordinary aspects of your being through the exercises of Freedom.

OUT OF BODY EXPERIENCE (OBE)

Prior to starting the exercises, take a moment to contemplate your current state of consciousness within the larger continuum. Imagine a radio dial where turning it changes stations, creating a continuum of consciousness. For example, when you are in a state of alert awareness, you focus on the present physical reality, which is like one station on the dial. However, at times, you might find your attention tuned into a different channel, like when you daydream on the border between wakefulness and sleep. The Gateway Experience employs the heavy sync to shift attention to specific states of consciousness, which might lead to experiences like the Out-of-Body Experience (OBE).

In OBEs, consciousness can either be localized or separated from the physical body. Sometimes, you may be aware of both your physical and nonphysical bodies simultaneously. OBEs can involve experiencing distant locations while being in your nonphysical body at the same time. In contrast, Remote Viewing (Freedom #2) allows consciousness to expand towards specific objectives or distant places by expanding immediate awareness.

There are no rigid rules or norms when it comes to perceiving nonphysical consciousness. Whether it's experienced as a body, sphere of light, or flowing energy, each individual's journey is unique. As you gain proficiency in experiencing consciousness as separate from the physical world, the method of perception becomes less crucial, and experiences might vary from one OBE to another. Any experience where consciousness is distinct from the physical body is considered an OBE, even if you are aware of your physical body while having an OBE.

During OBEs, thought and intention are tightly linked, and even fleeting thoughts can manifest quickly. As your experience grows, you'll learn to distinguish between thought and intent, enhancing your control over the OBE process. Reducing fear and physical habits can lead to more natural and freeing OBE experiences. Learning to create high-energy states, which can be achieved through The Gateway Experience, is crucial in developing OBE proficiency.

To prepare for OBE exercises in Freedom, practice various separation techniques. These exercises will help you explore the distinction between physical and nonphysical energies, providing valuable insights into your personal makeup and inducing OBEs. Experiment with different techniques until you find what feels comfortable. If you encounter stiffness or feel disconnected from your physical body, you can return to position C-1 by saying or thinking the number one and moving your fingers.

During the OBE process, the energy might build rapidly, leading to a quick separation with possible rushing sounds. Once you reach this point, you are in complete control of your adventure and experiences. The possibilities for exploration are vast and not limited by constraints or personal limitations.

Remember that fear is common for some people desiring OBEs. Utilize tools like the REBAL and EBT to ease fears and maintain a sense of safety during the OBE process. Let go of expectations and trust your higher self, expressing gratitude for whatever experience comes your way. Conscious OBEs might also occur during sleep, making the ability to perform this process consciously a valuable goal. Each person's OBE experience is unique, and with practice, you can gain more control and explore limitless possibilities.

During an Out-of-Body Experience (OBE), consciousness can either be localized or separated from one's physical body, depending on the situation. It is even possible for awareness to be focused in multiple locations simultaneously. For instance, one can maintain awareness of both the physical body and the nonphysical, or second, body simultaneously. Moreover, detachment from the second body might lead to a third localized awareness (as described in Robert Monroe's book, "Far Journeys").

OBEs often involve experiencing distant locations from one's physical body while being present in the nonphysical body at that distant location. In contrast, Remote Viewing (Freedom #2) involves expanding one's consciousness in a specific direction toward a particular objective. By doing so, individuals can envelop and become conscious of people, places, or events that are physically distant from their immediate awareness by expanding their consciousness.

There are distinct differences between physical and nonphysical reality. In the C-1 state, you have the option to decide whether a thought leads to action. However, during the early stages of OBE development, a thought can instantaneously transform into action. Even a fleeting thought about a person or location can swiftly transport you to that exact place. With practice, you will learn to differentiate between thought and intent, allowing you to reflect and consider your experiences during an OBE actively.

Because much of our thinking is influenced by habits, during an OBE, we might appear and behave similarly to how we do in our physical bodies. The perception of the second body can range from having limbs and a head to being a sphere of light or an indistinct mass of energy alongside the first body.

Fear and thinking habits play a significant role in OBEs. If one remains attached to physical reality during an OBE, a "reality shock" may arise—a fear of separation from one's physical self or body. Conversely, when one lets go of physical habits and embraces nonphysical energy experiences, OBEs become more natural, offering a sense of boundless freedom. Although OBEs can theoretically occur during sleep, mastering conscious control of this natural process is the ultimate exercise goal.

People have diverse experiences during OBEs. Some may not remember how they separated from or re-entered their physical bodies, while others use specific techniques. Our research suggests that achieving a high-energy state could lead to conscious OBEs. Thus, it is recommended to learn how to create high-energy states, which can be achieved through incorporating lessons from The Gateway Experience into your daily routine.

To progress further, practice various OBE separation techniques provided in Freedom. These exercises will reveal distinctions between physical and nonphysical energies, leading to a deeper understanding of your personal makeup and the induction of OBEs. Through patient and relaxed effort, you can explore these energies, gaining experience and knowledge on how to utilize them productively.

Experiment with different techniques until you find one that feels comfortable, and put it into practice. If you ever feel stiff or lose contact with your physical body during an OBE, you can always return to position C-1. Simply say or think the number one in your mind while moving the fingers of your right hand to become physically awake and alert once more.

The process of separation during an OBE can occur at incredible speed and with roaring or rushing sounds when energy suddenly and dramatically builds up. After reaching this point, you become solely responsible for the action, adventure, and experience of your OBE. You are free to explore the solar system, map terrains between physical and nonphysical realities, form connections with nonphysical entities, or simply fly over treetops to gain a sense of your surroundings. The possibilities are boundless, limited only by your self-imposed constraints and your desire to grow.

ABOUT FEAR-

Fear is a common aspect for some individuals who desire to experience out-of-body travel while simultaneously being excited of the prospect. Fortunately, you now possess knowledge of tools to help you cope with such fears. One technique involves putting your fears in a mental box, where you can detach from them during your out-of-body experiences. Additionally, include a reassuring and calming affirmation that your REBAL (Reference Energy Balloon) will accompany you, ensuring your safety and comfort throughout the journey. You can also request assistance in easing your fears, envisioning your Energy Balloon as a two-lane highway that can transport you away and return you safely to your starting point.

It is crucial to release any expectations you might have about your out-of-body experiences. Trust your higher self to guide you towards what is best for you, and maintain a sense of gratitude for whatever experiences come your way. Remember that you can always return to your fully conscious state by simply thinking the number one and moving your fingers back and forth.

As you experiment with various separation techniques during the Wave Three exercises, you may discover that certain techniques work better for you than others. Alternatively, you may find that energy builds up naturally, leading to a sudden separation while in a relaxed state. In such cases, allow the audios to guide you along the continuum.

Practice is essential in developing proficiency in out-of-body experiences. Your repeated efforts and experience will grant you more control over the process, allowing you to tailor the adventure according to your preferences. You have the freedom to explore the solar system, map the terrains between physical and nonphysical realms, establish relationships with nonphysical entities, or simply soar over nearby treetops. The possibilities are boundless and determined only by your unique characteristics and the direction you wish to take in your life's journey.

Freedom #1: Liftoff

This exercise is designed to help you achieve a state of complete calm and comfort, dissociating your perspective from your physical body. This exercise will be most effective for you if you have already become familiar with the REBAL (Reference Energy Balloon) during your training. If needed, refer back to page 25 of the Discovery instructions to refresh your memory on the REBAL's capabilities.

During Liftoff, you will work on getting your REBAL into optimal condition. You will then practice the sensation of floating a short distance away from your physical body while maintaining awareness within yourself. It is essential to understand that this exercise does not involve physically separating from your body but rather provides you with the perception of movement and action.

As you perform Liftoff, imagine yourself floating upward, akin to flying or soaring, without any effort. Visualize it as if you are standing in an elevator, gently rising without exertion, and feel yourself relaxing and settling down. Instead of focusing on your physical body, shift your attention to the essence of your nonphysical energy.

Consistent practice of Liftoff will familiarize you with this technique and make it second nature to you. Moreover, it will instill a sense of confidence that you can easily and safely return to your physical body whenever you wish. This knowledge will empower you to venture further away from your physical body for more extended periods in subsequent exercises.

Liftoff not only serves as a valuable practice tool but also brings a sense of enjoyment to your exploration of nonphysical consciousness. By incorporating this exercise into your routine, you will gain a unique perspective and enhance your ability to navigate the realms of nonphysical energy with ease. So, continue to practice Liftoff until you feel comfortable and proficient with the technique.

Freedom #2: Remote Viewing

In Freedom 2, you will learn a method to extend your consciousness and perceive distant people, places, and events. The process involves placing your EBT (Energy Balloon Technique) at the center of your consciousness and allowing it to stretch or flow out to the target you wish to perceive. When you are in Focus 10, your perception of space is different, and the awareness of a location or person can merge with your consciousness in unexpected ways. It's akin to calling out to or reaching out to the target from within yourself.

In Focus 10, time and space are not limited as in C-1 (your normal waking state). Therefore, when remote viewing, you only need to consider time and space to determine the most appropriate moment to immerse your awareness in the target location.

An example from a Gateway session in Richmond, Virginia, involved a participant who "saw" a distinctive red car parked in front of the building. Although he couldn't find the car during his hasty search, he was surprised to see the red car exactly as he had perceived it earlier when he returned after lunch. This illustrates the convenience of remote viewing while also emphasizing the importance of being time-conscious.

To practice remote viewing, you can experiment with a friend who chooses a specific location in their home or office where a target object can be placed. Surround the object with your awareness and explore how your perceptions work. Notice whether you are more likely to perceive geometric shapes, colors, or textures, and try to understand how the function of an object might affect your ability to resonate with it.

It's important to avoid interpreting data sets and instead focus on describing what you perceive accurately. Mistakes in interpretation can lead to incorrect assessments of the target. For instance, in the book "Mind Reach" by Harold Puthoff and Russell Targ, one subject mistook a cement rectangle filled with water for a swimming pool, resulting in a miss during the exercise.

The stories of portals leading to remote viewing experiences are intriguing and can teach us about our assumptions, perceptions, and how they shape our experiences. For instance, a person became disoriented in a blizzard while trying to find a target concealed in an almost empty flour sack. Another person saw a quarter moon in broad daylight while attempting to look through a paper bag, thinking it was ridiculous, but the actual target was a lemon wedge in a teacup.

Remote viewing challenges our assumptions and deepens our understanding of perceptions and consciousness. By practicing remote viewing, you can enhance your ability to perceive distant targets and gain valuable insights into the nature of consciousness itself.

This exercise will allow you to demonstrate and apply the energy tools you have learned. Before performing the experiment, familiarize yourself with the technique by listening to the audio tape. Here are the steps to prepare for the experiment:

1. Obtain a White Paper Bag: The white paper bag serves as the target container, and its clean and unstained state ensures that there are no distracting associations or biases with the object placed inside it.

2. Set up the Area: Creating a separate space away from where you'll listen to the exercise ensures that you are not influenced by your immediate surroundings during the remote viewing process. This isolation helps to maintain the integrity of your perceptions.

3. Choose a Friend as a Test Partner: Selecting a trustworthy friend to be your test partner adds an element of validation to the experiment. The fact that they are physically separated from you demonstrates that remote viewing transcends distance.

4. Plan the Target Object: Both you and your friend should agree on a specific object or photograph to be placed inside the white bag. It is crucial that you remain completely unaware of the target to avoid any preconceived notions or biases.

5. Schedule and Duration: Set a specific time for the experiment, aligning it with the length of the remote viewing exercise. Allowing enough time for

note-taking and reflection afterward will enhance your learning experience.

6. Use the EBT Technique: The Energy Balloon Technique (EBT) is a valuable tool to help you perform remote viewing. By incorporating the EBT, you can enhance your focus and energy awareness during the exercise.

7. Record Impressions and Feelings: After completing the remote viewing exercise, document your impressions and feelings about the target object. This introspection helps you understand your perceptions and emotions during the process.

8. Communicate with Your Friend: Contact your friend to share the information you gathered during the remote viewing. Prompt feedback enables you to assess the accuracy of your results and refine your abilities.

9. Learn from Mistakes and Successes: Analyze any errors in your perceptions and try to understand the reasons behind them. Also, take note of any accurate conclusions you reached to build confidence in your remote viewing skills.

10. Keep Track of Results: Maintain a record of your remote viewing sessions to identify patterns and progress over time. By reviewing your experiences, you can gain insights into your strengths and areas for improvement.

11. Incorporate Abilities into Daily Life: As you develop your remote viewing abilities, try to integrate them into your daily routine. This practice

encourages a more continuous exploration of your awareness.

12. Embrace Understanding over Failure: In the context of remote viewing, there are no psychic failures. Every experience, whether perceived as a success or not, contributes to a deeper understanding of your consciousness and its potential.

Remember, remote viewing is an ongoing process of learning and growth. Each session provides an opportunity to explore the boundaries of your consciousness and expand your understanding of the nonphysical dimensions. As you become more adept at remote viewing, you may find it beneficial to experiment with new applications of this technique in various aspects of your life.

Freedom #3: Vectors

Freedom #3: Vectors is a unique exercise that introduces you to a three-dimensional system of reference points to aid in exploring nonphysical energy. While nonphysical energy is not limited to conventional time and space, the "Vectors" exercise uses the analogy of a clock face to provide you with a sense of direction and orientation.

Clock Face Analogy: In this exercise, you imagine a clock face with the time starting at twelve o'clock just above your head, six o'clock just below your feet, three o'clock just outside your left hip, and nine o'clock just beyond your right hip. The first step involves moving your perception around this clock face to explore different directions and locations. You'll observe and note any emotions or interesting features as you navigate through these points.

Rotation and Movement: The second part of the exercise involves rotating the clock face ninety degrees in the opposite direction. The positions of twelve, three, six, and nine change accordingly. Your third eye aligns with the number three, and the number nine is behind you, just beyond your waistline.

Forward and Outward Movement: In the third and final part, you'll be guided forward and outward to a new three o'clock position just in front of your feet. Then, you'll move outward and upward to the new nine o'clock position beyond your waist and hips, starting from twelve o'clock above your head. The movement culminates as you return to the twelve o'clock position at the top of your head.

Tracking Changes in Awareness: Throughout the exercise, you'll observe any significant changes in your personal awareness and note how they relate to the time on the clock face. As your proficiency grows, you may establish new vectors, creating additional exploration opportunities within this three-dimensional pattern. Pay close attention to any vectors that feel comfortable, stimulating, or provide valuable information, and record them in your notes.

Repetition and Proficiency: It's normal to repeat the exercise several times to become proficient with it. The more you use this technique, the more effective it becomes. With practice, the pattern can become automatic in any exploration, enabling you to navigate nonphysical energy with greater ease and accuracy.

Remember, the purpose of "Vectors" is to provide you with a framework to orient yourself in nonphysical energy and explore different directions. As you progress through the exercises, you may develop additional extensions and adapt the technique to suit your preferences and needs. Keep an open mind and be receptive to new experiences and insights as you continue your journey of self-discovery through nonphysical exploration.

Freedom #4: Five Questions

In Freedom #4, you will embark on a profound journey of self-discovery by seeking answers to five fundamental questions. This exercise is the beginning of a process that you can incorporate regularly to gain deeper insights into your existence and purpose. During Focus 12, you will be asked to contemplate the following questions:

1. Who am I?

This question delves into the essence of your being, beyond your physical identity and societal roles. It seeks to connect you with your true self, exploring the depths of your consciousness and spiritual nature.

2. Where and who was I before I entered this physical being?

In this question, you are encouraged to explore the concept of existence beyond your current physical life. It invites you to consider your existence before this lifetime and to explore the idea of the soul's journey through different states of being.

3. What is my purpose for this existence in physical matter reality?

This question prompts you to reflect on the purpose and significance of your current physical existence. It encourages you to understand your life's mission and the lessons you are meant to learn during this earthly experience.

4. What action can I now take to serve this purpose best?

Here, you are asked to contemplate the actions and choices that align with your life's purpose. It emphasizes the importance of living intentionally and taking steps to fulfill your higher calling.

5. What is the most important message that I can receive and understand at this point in my existence?

The final question invites you to be receptive to receiving guidance or insights that are most relevant to your current state of being. It encourages openness to messages from your inner wisdom or higher sources.

During the Focus 12 exercise, the answers to these questions may not come in the form of spoken or written words. Instead, you may receive them as images, feelings, intuitions, or other nonverbal modes of perception. It is normal to experience these responses, and it is your responsibility to interpret and translate them into meaningful insights.

Remember that this process may require patience and multiple attempts. If you need further clarity or if the answers are not immediately clear, don't hesitate to repeat the exercise. Through this exploration, you will gradually gain a more profound understanding of your true self and your purpose in this existence. Embrace the journey of self-discovery with an open heart and mind, and allow the process to unfold organically.

Freedom #5: Energy Food

In Freedom #5, you will learn a powerful method for restoring depleted energy in a way that goes beyond traditional methods such as eating. The exercise will teach you how to draw energy from the nonphysical realms that you have been exploring throughout The Gateway Experience. This process will allow you to nourish yourself and revitalize your energy levels in a unique and profound manner.

This exercise serves as a practice session, an encodement of the process, rather than an immediate real-world application. After completing the exercise, you will have the opportunity to apply this newfound skill in your physical reality (C-1). By extending your hands outward, palms up, you will perceive, absorb, and store energy in various ways.

Using this energy restoration method alongside other tools in The Gateway Experience will enhance its effectiveness. As you practice, you will find that some individuals can retain and utilize this skill after just one session, while others may require two or three sessions to fully integrate it into their abilities.

After each session, it is advisable to test the method to evaluate your progress. Pay attention to how you feel and whether you experience a sense of increased energy and vitality as a result of this practice. With consistent practice, you will likely notice improvements in your ability to restore energy.

Initially, you may use a physical representation, such as masking tape, to help you focus during the exercise.

However, as you become more proficient, you will no longer require external aids. The ability to draw and store energy will become a natural part of your being, seamlessly integrated into your personality and capabilities.

Remember, the energy you explore and utilize during these exercises is not limited to physical sources. By tapping into the nonphysical realms and understanding the nature of energy, you can access a vast reservoir of revitalizing power. Embrace this practice with an open mind and heart, and let it become an empowering tool in your journey of self-discovery and personal growth.

Freedom #6: First-Stage Separation

"First-Stage Separation" is a significant milestone that empowers you to gain conscious control over your entire energy system, encompassing both your physical body and nonphysical energies. The earlier exercises were meticulously designed to facilitate an easier and more enjoyable experience with this particular exercise. Here, we will explore five different methods of disassociating from your physical body, guiding you through this transformative process.

The primary objective is to develop a clearer distinction between your physical and nonphysical energies as you progress. By achieving this separation of awareness from these energies, you will gain the ability to localize your focus more effectively either in your physical body or in your second body, thereby reaping numerous benefits. As with other tools in this program, you are encouraged to choose the method that resonates most comfortably with you. Alternatively, feel free to combine multiple approaches in a way that suits your unique preferences. Rest assured that each of these methods has been successfully employed by numerous participants over the years.

Remember, this is a journey of exploration and discovery, and there's no rush to master all the techniques immediately. Allow yourself the time and patience to progress at your own pace, and with each step, you will gain a deeper understanding of your energy system and consciousness. Embrace the process, and you'll unlock new realms of awareness and self-discovery.

Throughout your training in these techniques, you will be gently guided through the following procedures:

LOGROLLING.

To perform the "Logrolling" technique, focus your attention on the nonphysical energy within your physical body. Imagine this energy as a log floating in water, and slowly and gently rotate it within your body. Allow yourself to feel the sensation of this rotational movement, as if there were an axis running through the length of your body.

As you continue the rotation, pay attention to any sensations or feelings that arise. You might sense a release of what seems like "surface tension" as the energy begins to move more freely. When you experience this release, be sure to let go of any pressure you might have been exerting on the rotational movement. If you hold on to the pressure, you may find yourself spinning faster than you intended.

You may notice that the rotation is partial at first, perhaps only 90 to 180 degrees. Don't worry; this is a natural part of the process. As you stabilize this "out of phase" condition between your physical and nonphysical energies, you will gain the ability to "peel" out of your physical body.

To perform the "peeling" process, continue moving outward and turning over, separating your second body from your physical body. This is a gradual process, and you should feel a sense of detachment from your physical form. As you peel out of your body, you will experience a new level of awareness in your second body.

To reintegrate with the physical world, simply rotate your second body until it aligns with the physical world once more. You might feel a subtle click or shift as you reintegrate into the physical realm.

Remember, this technique requires patience and practice. It's essential to maintain a calm and focused state of mind throughout the process. With time and dedication, you will develop greater control over your nonphysical energies and gain a deeper understanding of your consciousness.

POLE.

In the second method, envision your second body as a rigid pole rather than a flexible log. Slowly and deliberately, imagine your second body being expelled from your physical body. This process begins at your feet and gradually progresses through your legs, waist, abdomen, chest, shoulders, and finally standing upright at a 90-degree angle to your physical body.

Throughout this process, keep in mind that your only point of contact with your physical body is where your energy feet are still within touching distance of your physical feet. As you maintain this pivotal point, gradually move your nonphysical energy upward and away from your physical body, starting with your head first.

With focused intent, continue the upward movement until you are fully upright and only your energy feet remain in contact with your physical feet. At this point, your second body will be separated from your physical body.

The key to this method is to maintain a sense of rigidity and solidity in your second body as it moves away from your physical body. By visualizing it as a rigid pole and following the gradual expulsion process, you can achieve a complete separation of your nonphysical energy from your physical form.

As with any technique, practice and patience are essential for refining your ability to perform this method effectively. With time and dedication, you will become more adept at controlling your energy system and achieving conscious separation from your physical body.

FLOWING

"Flowing" is a method of projecting your non-physical energies through the top of your head in a manner similar to a cloud, fog, or a thin spray of gas. Once separated, these energies often naturally take the form of a replica of your physical body. From this point, you have various options: you can use your EBT to move away, float within your REBAL, practice your vectors, or utilize any other tools you have learned during your training.

The process of separation is straightforward - simply hold the intention to separate your second body from your physical body. This focused desire for separation is sufficient to achieve complete disassociation. Should you wish to return to your physical body, you can use the C-1 encoding technique. For those who are still in touch with their physical bodies, simply reverse your intention and tilt backward to reintegrate with it.

With practice and familiarity, you will find this method to be a fluid and natural way to project your non-physical energies and achieve conscious separation. Remember to approach the process with a calm and focused mindset, allowing the separation to occur smoothly and effortlessly. As you gain more experience with this technique, you will have the freedom to explore and utilize the vast potential of your non-physical consciousness.

BACKING AWAY

"Backing Away" is a method that involves a deliberate and gradual movement of your non-physical body away from your physical body. The goal is to create a sense of distance and separation between the two energy systems. This technique allows you to explore the non-physical realms while still maintaining a connection to your physical body.

To begin, focus your attention on your non-physical energy, which exists within your physical body. Visualize yourself slowly and deliberately backing away from your physical form. You may imagine this as a gentle and fluid movement, as if you are stepping back from your body.

As you back away, you might feel a sensation of sinking down through the surface you are lying on, indicating the detachment from your physical body. Take your time with this process, ensuring that you are comfortable and relaxed throughout.

Once you have achieved a sense of distance from your physical body, you can experiment with turning away and moving in different directions using the techniques you learned in the "Vectors" exercise. The ability to establish reference points and navigate in three-dimensional space will come in handy during this exploration.

It's essential to maintain a clear intention and focus during this practice. By desiring to separate your non-physical body from your physical body, you will enhance the effectiveness of the technique. Additionally, knowing that you can always return to your physical body by reversing your intention and gently reconnecting is reassuring.

As you gain proficiency in "Backing Away," you will be able to explore further and more comfortably. This technique, like others in The Gateway Experience, empowers you to have conscious control over your energy system and broaden your understanding of the non-physical aspects of existence. Regular practice and patience will aid you in achieving successful out-of-body experiences and personal growth on your journey of exploration.

FLOATING

The final technique, "Floating," involves imagining the pleasant sensation of floating upward, akin to a cloud or kite. When you emotionally desire this experience, your non-physical energy will respond accordingly. However, it's important to gradually remove or control the emotion so that other aspects of your being can direct your experiences in the most beneficial manner.

Like the previous techniques, "Floating" requires consistent practice. Engaging in regular practice will heighten your awareness of the out-of-body processes and dynamics. You can find detailed descriptions and explanations of these techniques in the book "Journeys Out of the Body" by Robert Monroe.

During out-of-body experiences, some individuals may experience excitement, causing a premature return to their physical body. To mitigate this, you can employ the techniques learned to develop patience and relaxed effort, thus reducing the likelihood of abrupt returns. Preparedness and self-control will enable you to fully appreciate and embrace your out-of-body experiences when they occur.

Always remember that you have complete control over the process, and you can return to your physical body at any time. A helpful method for immediate reintegration with your physical body is visualizing a specific body part, such as the fingers, and gently moving it. This triggers the process of returning to full physical awareness. Engaging in activities like walking or showering further aids in completing the reintegration process. Understanding this "quick return" procedure reinforces your sense of independence and assurance.

It is essential to recognize that the effects of using these energy tools are cumulative. Proficiency in one skill enhances and improves your ability to use others. Perseverance is key, as mastering The Gateway Experience, like any skill, demands dedication and practice over time. With continued commitment and determination, you can unlock the profound potential of conscious exploration and personal growth offered by The Gateway Experience.

Wave IV: Adventure

During your non-physical exploration, the Discovery exercises assisted you in establishing a safe and comfortable foundation for further exploration. The Threshold exercises, on the tenth day, provided you with additional tools for directing and controlling non-physical energy while in the energy state of Concentration, which you can now use to your advantage. Through practice and separation of your non-physical form from your physical body, you have achieved freedom in exercise number twelve.

Now, with Adventure, you have the opportunity to direct and control new experiences, tap into innovative ideas, develop new capabilities, and embark on exciting exploration opportunities in new and unfamiliar locations. These exercises will enable you to express your consciousness dynamically while engaging in personally controlled and directed adventures.

Please note that before beginning Adventure, it is essential to have completed all previous Gateway Experience Waves of Change exercises. These exercises are designed to build upon one another, and it is recommended not to proceed with Adventure unless you have prior experience with the previous exercises. This ensures that you are adequately prepared and equipped for the challenges and experiences that Adventure will offer.

Adventure #1: One Year Patterning

In Adventure #1: One Year Patterning, you will embark on a transformative journey of envisioning and shaping your desired self and life one year into the future. This exercise builds upon the concepts and techniques introduced in Threshold #3: One-Month Patterning, with the main difference being the extended time span and the deeper understanding of your ability to harness the power of expanded consciousness.

Similar to One-Month Patterning, the first step is to carefully consider and define how you want to be in a year's time. Reflect on your goals, aspirations, and the changes you wish to manifest in various aspects of your life. The guidelines for setting intentions and directing your consciousness remain the same, but with one-year patterning, you have the advantage of a longer time frame to work with.

The key principles of setting clear intentions, aligning your thoughts and emotions, and releasing any doubts or limitations still apply. However, in One Year Patterning, you have the opportunity to explore and plan for more comprehensive and long-term transformations. You can delve deeper into your personal growth, career aspirations, relationships, health, and other life areas, allowing for a more holistic and far-reaching impact.

Additionally, the extended duration of one-year patterning enables you to dream bigger and explore the possibilities of your future self more expansively. You can visualize and embody the person you wish to become, experiencing the fulfillment of your desires and the realization of your potential in vivid detail.

The increased time span also offers a chance to cultivate greater trust in the process of manifestation. As you progress through the Gateway Experience and gain a deeper understanding of your ability to harness the power of expanded consciousness, you can approach one-year patterning with heightened confidence and gratitude. Trusting in the unfolding of your intentions becomes more profound as you witness the transformative effects of your thoughts and emotions over an extended period.

Before commencing this exercise, it is essential to prepare a comprehensive and detailed plan for the pattern you wish to create. Take the lessons learned from One-Month Patterning and apply them to design a roadmap for your one-year journey of growth and self-realization.

Remember, the power of intention and conscious manifestation remains a central theme, whether in one-month or one-year patterning. You have the freedom and flexibility to adapt the techniques to suit your needs and preferences while utilizing the accumulated wisdom and skills acquired throughout your Gateway Experience.

In conclusion, Adventure #1: One Year Patterning offers an expanded canvas for creating your desired future self and life. Building on the foundation laid in Threshold #3, this exercise empowers you to dream big, set ambitious goals, and embrace the transformative potential of your consciousness over an extended period. Trust, confidence, and gratitude play an even more significant role as you venture into this year-long journey of self-discovery and personal growth.

Adventure #2: Five Messages

In Adventure #2: Five Messages, you will be guided to receive five important messages, presented in order of their significance for you at this time. These messages are not typically conveyed through conventional verbal means; instead, they are transmitted through nonverbal communication, utilizing the heightened perception skills you have developed throughout The Gateway Experience. The exercise emphasizes the importance of receptivity, as it is crucial to refrain from analyzing or interpreting the messages while in the process of receiving them.

To embark on this journey, all you need is an open mind, a sense of gratitude, and a heightened sensitivity to your perceptions, just as you have been cultivating in your previous experiences. The exercise takes place in the Focus 12 state, a synchronized and expanded state of awareness.

The five messages will come to you in a natural flow, without the need for any specific preparation. The key is to be receptive and allow the messages to unfold without the interference of left-brain functions such as analysis or interpretation. These functions can disrupt the seamless flow of nonverbal communication and the synchronization of your Focus 12 state.

It is essential to remember that the true understanding and interpretation of the messages come after the exercise is completed. Attempting to analyze or interpret the messages during the process can disrupt the flow and hinder your ability to receive them fully.

As you engage in Adventure #2, you may find it beneficial to revisit the guidelines provided in Threshold #4: Freedom Four, as it offers additional suggestions and insights to enhance your experience.

Approaching this adventure with openness, gratitude, and a receptive mindset will enable you to tap into the deeper realms of consciousness and receive the valuable messages meant specifically for you at this point in your journey. Trust in the process and the wisdom of your higher self as you embark on this transformative exploration.

Adventure #3: Free Flow 12

In Adventure #3: Free Flow 12, you will be equipped with eight beacon guideposts, personal reference points that will aid you in planning and executing systematic explorations to your desired destinations. By setting a clear purpose or destination before beginning the exercise, you can avoid drifting into a state of sleep or entering a dream-like state. Expressing gratitude for the information or guidance you receive during your explorations will deepen your connection and open doors to further expansion of your journeys.

This exercise offers tremendous flexibility, allowing you to repeat it as many times as you desire. With a carefully chosen backdrop, you can embark on planned and systematic explorations in any direction you choose. It is essential to establish your objectives before starting to maintain focus and intention throughout the process.

Your responsibility lies in completing the preparatory process and then transitioning from Focus 10 to Focus 12. Upon reaching Focus 12, you will encounter the beacon guideposts, serving as your starting points. The non-intrusive sound of these guideposts will gently remind you of your location and identity, granting you the freedom to explore extensively without the fear of becoming disoriented or losing sight of your objectives.

Adventure #3 empowers you to embrace boundless exploration and discovery, guided by your purpose and intentions. As you delve deeper into the realms of consciousness, remember to stay mindful and receptive, expressing gratitude for the insights and experiences that unfold during your journey. The more you practice this exercise, the broader the horizons of your exploration will become, enriching your understanding and connection with the vastness of consciousness. Enjoy the wonders of Free Flow 12 and the limitless opportunities it presents for personal growth and self-discovery.

Adventure #4: Non-Verbal Communication

Non-Verbal Communication (NVC) introduces you to a profound method of interaction between different realities and energy systems. NVC goes beyond the conventional notion of body language and becomes a comprehensive means of expression that occurs within the mind and in mind-to-mind exchanges. Throughout your Gateway Experience journey, you have encountered glimpses of NVC in various exercises, dream states, vibrations, light, and emotional sensations.

NVC is distinct from verbal communication in its nature and process. While both forms involve perceiving data and translating it to convey meaning, NVC operates on a deeper level of awareness, tapping into non-physical perceptions. Dreams, for instance, are predominantly composed of NVC experiences. As you explore further, you will build your NVC vocabulary, recognizing and understanding unique forms of perception that you encounter in your non-physical explorations.

To fully harness the power of NVC, apply it immediately in your adventures. This exercise serves as your primary lesson in non-verbal communication. The tools and methods of perception you have developed in previous exercises are now ripe for application. Dedicate yourself to cultivating this method of total communication, exploring its nuances and deepening your understanding. As you practice,

323

you will witness the transformative potential of NVC in your interactions and explorations.

Through Adventure #4, you gain the ability to communicate and interact beyond conventional language, tapping into the richness of non-physical perceptions. Embrace the possibilities of NVC, experiment with different forms of communication, and let your confidence in this extraordinary skill grow. As you progress, you may find that words are not always necessary to convey profound meanings and connections. So, immerse yourself in the art of non-verbal communication and unlock new dimensions of understanding and connection in your journey through consciousness.

Adventure #5: NVC II

In this additional piece of NVC instruction, you will find that the techniques of translation and conceptualization become more refined and apparent as you progress. As you delve deeper into the realm of non-verbal communication, you will discover that your abilities to perceive and interpret meaning expand significantly across all states of being.

With dedicated practice and exploration, you will become more adept at translating and understanding the subtle nuances of NVC. Just like learning any language, the more you immerse yourself in its usage, the more fluent and proficient you become. As you advance in your NVC journey, you will find that your range of perception expands, allowing you to pick up on even the most subtle cues and energetic expressions from different realities and energy systems.

NVC offers a profound way of connecting and communicating with others, whether in non-physical realms or in everyday life. It goes beyond words, allowing you to tap into the underlying essence of emotions, intentions, and energies that might be challenging to convey through conventional language.

As you progress in your mastery of NVC, you may notice that your interactions with the world around you deepen and become more meaningful. Your heightened perception will not only enrich your personal experiences but also enable you to empathize with others on a deeper level. NVC can enhance your ability to understand and respond to the unspoken messages and emotions of those around you, fostering more authentic and harmonious connections.

Remember, the journey of developing NVC is ongoing, and there is always more to explore and learn. As you continue to practice and apply NVC in your life and throughout your Gateway Experience, you will discover the limitless potential of this extraordinary form of communication. Embrace this opportunity to expand your consciousness and connect with the essence of existence beyond the confines of verbal language.

Adventure #6: ComPoint

ComPoint, short for Communications Point, is a unique state of consciousness that you have the ability to enter and exit at will. This adventure invites you to actively engage in creating an environment that fosters communication and interaction with various energy systems and entities.

Imagine a space where communication flows effortlessly and where you can gather information, connect with others, or simply observe events and activities. This environment can be tailored to your preferences and needs. It could be a cutting-edge computer station, allowing you to interface with vast knowledge databases, a serene garden with comfortable seating to engage in tranquil exchanges, or a cozy log cabin where you can share cherished conversations with dear friends. The choice is yours, and the possibilities are endless.

Through your growing proficiency in non-verbal communication (NVC), you can utilize ComPoint to expand your NVC vocabulary. Reach out to others, exchange ideas, and bid farewell while expressing gratitude in various situations. With each interaction, your understanding of NVC deepens, and you become more adept at connecting with different energy systems and intelligences.

One of the most remarkable aspects of ComPoint is its accessibility. You can effortlessly access this state of consciousness whenever you wish. As a result, it serves as a convenient meeting place for connecting with virtual friends or gathering with like-minded individuals.

In ComPoint, you will experience a sense of interconnectedness and unity, transcending the limitations of conventional communication. Through this extraordinary adventure, you will expand your awareness of the vastness of existence and your place within it. Embrace the potential for profound experiences and transformative encounters as you explore the boundless realms of ComPoint.

Wave V: Exploring

Welcome to Wave 4 of the Gateway Experience! As you listen to these exercises, you may notice that they are comprised of musical sounds and Hemi-Sync® signals. However, what you are actually experiencing are the Focus 10 and Focus 12 processes presented in a different form. This Meta music has been carefully composed to enhance your nonverbal communication (NVC) skills. Through these exercises, you will be guided using the methods for reaching Focus 10 and Focus 12 that you have already learned. There are no verbal instructions; instead, the process is entirely driven by your mental direction.

With the assistance of this Meta music, you will learn to achieve your goals and create experiences without the need for external guidance. You will be in complete control of your journey, deciding where you want to explore and what you want to experience. Changes in the frequencies of the Hemi-Sync signals will guide you into different states of consciousness, facilitating your progression through the familiar preparatory process.

By this point in your Gateway Experience training, you have developed the knowledge and skills to control which Focus level you enter. The Focus 10 and Focus 12 Hemi-Sync® signals will aid you in reaching these levels for the first two Exploring exercises. After that, you will deliberately choose the Focus level that feels most comfortable for each individual exercise in the following Exploring exercises. For instance, you may find that Focus 10 is most effective for remote viewing, using your EBT, or practicing out-of-body procedures, while Focus 12 might be the optimal choice for patterning, problem-solving, or seeking guidance.

It is essential that you have completed all previous Gateway Experience Waves of Change exercises before using these exercises, as they build directly on the techniques and information learned in the earlier waves.

In Wave 4, you will reacquaint yourself with Focus 12, the state of expanded awareness. Following that, two additional Focus 12 exercises will help you further develop your intuitive abilities. You will have the opportunity to connect with and experience the feeling of intuitive knowing, as well as address any limiting beliefs or obstacles that may hinder your trust in your intuitive self.

From the familiar state of Focus 12, you will be introduced to Focus 15, the "no time" state—where you simply exist, transcending the limitations of your physical senses. Through Hemi-Sync® signals, you will expand your consciousness and connect with the source of your intuition. This leads to a powerful state of creation and manifestation in Focus 15 before culminating in a free flow Focus 15 exercise.

We encourage you to practice the verbal cues you learn in Wave 4, allowing you to repeat your experiences without relying on the exercises. As you engage in these explorations, you will find that with practice, it becomes easier to access and navigate these extraordinary states of consciousness.

Exploring #1: Advanced Focus 12

In Exploring #1—Advanced Focus 12, you will revisit the state of Focus 12, which is a state of expanded awareness. This exercise offers an excellent opportunity for more profound and in-depth explorations of the self. As you return to Focus 12, you will strengthen and reinforce your familiarity with this highly beneficial state of mind.

Once in Focus 12, you are free to explore and roam around. This state allows you to perceive using your nonphysical senses, granting you the opportunity to establish new patterns for your life or reestablish communication channels with your nonphysical friends, if you have encountered any during your previous Gateway Experience journeys.

Engaging in a mutual exchange of information during this exercise is a wonderful way to enhance your nonverbal communication skills. As you give and receive information in this nonphysical realm, you will find yourself becoming more adept at understanding and conveying messages without relying on spoken words.

Use this exercise as an opportunity to delve deeper into your inner world and expand your consciousness. By practicing in Focus 12, you will further develop your ability to navigate this expanded state of awareness, opening the doors to profound insights and self-discovery.

Exploring #2: Discovering Intuition

In Exploring #2—Discovering Intuition, you will build upon your experience in the Focus 12 state of expanded awareness to develop your intuitive abilities. This exercise will guide you in connecting with the feeling or feelings that are associated with intuitive knowing—those instances when you simply know or understand something without conscious thought.

During the exercise, you will identify this unique and personal indicator of your intuition in action. This feeling will serve as a reliable compass, guiding you in recognizing intuitive insights and understanding. Additionally, you will learn a verbal cue that you can use whenever you desire to gain complete and clear comprehension.

Regular practice is key to fostering and strengthening your intuitive abilities. As you exercise your intuition regularly, you will become more attuned to this innate aspect of yourself. Trusting and relying on your intuition will become second nature, enriching your decision-making process and empowering you to tap into the deeper wisdom within you. Embrace this journey of self-discovery and intuition, and you will unlock new realms of understanding and insight.

Exploring #3: Exploring Intuition

In Exploring #3—Exploring Intuition, you will continue to delve into the realm of intuition by utilizing the Focus 12 state, which is readily available to you during this session. The HemiSync® signals will support you in expanding your consciousness beyond the confines of your five physical senses, granting you access to deeper aspects of life.

As you embark on this exploration, set the intention to understand and fully embrace yourself as an intuitive being. Connect with the source of your intuition, seeking to gain a deeper understanding and knowledge of your innate intuitive abilities. Throughout this process, be open to receiving insights and revelations that will help you recognize and trust your intuitive self more fully.

If you encounter any limiting beliefs or obstacles during this exercise, consider enlisting the assistance of a professional who can help you identify and address them. By acknowledging and releasing these hindrances, you can liberate yourself from their constraints and enhance your intuitive abilities.

Before concluding the session and returning to your physical waking consciousness, take a moment to express gratitude for the trust and confidence you have placed in your intuitive self. Acknowledge the significance of this journey of self-discovery, and honor the wisdom that resides within you. Embrace this experience as a stepping stone to a more profound connection with your intuition, and recognize the transformative power it holds in shaping your life.

Exploring #4: Intro to Focus 15

Intro to Focus 15, you will journey beyond the now familiar Focus 12 state and enter a new realm known as Focus 15—the state of "no time." In this state, the constraints of time cease to exist, granting you a profound sense of freedom from temporal limitations.

As you transition into Focus 15, you will experience a state of being where time no longer holds sway over your energy body. It is a space where you can effortlessly move in and out of, unrestricted by the conventional boundaries of time and space. The transition between Focus 12 and Focus 15 will be smooth and seamless, allowing you to explore this boundless state of consciousness with ease.

Throughout this exercise, you will move back and forth between Focus 12 and Focus 15, becoming more acquainted and comfortable with the unique sensations and experiences that arise in the state of "no time." By navigating these transitions repeatedly, you will develop a deeper understanding and connection to the concept of timelessness.

As the session nears its conclusion, you will be gently guided back to Focus 12, and then once more to Focus 15, before being brought back into full waking consciousness. This process will aid in solidifying your familiarity and ease with the state of "no time."

Embrace this journey into Focus 15 as an opportunity to expand your awareness beyond the confines of time and to gain new insights into the nature of consciousness. As you continue to explore this state, you may discover a profound sense of liberation and a deeper connection to the timeless essence of your being. Trust in the process and allow yourself to surrender to the experience of timelessness.

Exploring #5: Mission 15

The Acts of Creation and Manifestation, you will delve deeper into the profound state of Focus 15—a state of complete stillness and pure being. Within this state, you will uncover the power of creation and manifestation, opening up extraordinary possibilities for intentional transformation.

As you enter the state of Focus 15, you will experience a profound sense of inner stillness, free from the distractions of external stimuli. It is within this space of serene presence that you will connect with the boundless energy of the "ALL THAT IS." This vast cosmic consciousness holds the potential for infinite creation and manifestation.

With the guidance of Hemi-Sync® signals, you will learn to access this potent creative energy within Focus 15. You will understand how your intentions have the power to set in motion the creative forces of the universe. By aligning your focus with your desires, you can initiate the process of manifestation.

Throughout this exercise, you will be introduced to a verbal cue that will serve as a powerful tool for invoking change and materializing your dreams in your waking life. This cue will act as a bridge between your intentions in Focus 15 and the physical reality you seek to manifest.

Embrace this opportunity to explore the realm of creation and manifestation, for within Focus 15 lies the potential to bring about significant shifts in your life. Trust in your ability to harness the creative energies of the universe and be receptive to the profound transformations that may unfold as a result of your focused intention. As you gain confidence in this process, you will realize the true power of your thoughts and intentions in shaping your reality. Use this newfound understanding to pave the way for a life filled with purpose, abundance, and fulfillment.

Exploring #6: Exploring Focus 15

As you embark on the final adventure of Wave V, you are now well-acquainted with the profound state of Focus 15—the realm of "no time," where the constraints of linear time dissolve, and the essence of pure being prevails. In Exercise 6, you are presented with a precious opportunity to delve even deeper into the wonders of this extraordinary state.

Within the tranquil abode of Focus 15, you will encounter boundless freedom to explore the vast expanse of consciousness. With no limitations or boundaries, you are invited to venture into uncharted territories of awareness. Your intuitive faculties may guide you to new insights and revelations, allowing you to connect with the infinite well of creativity within.

As you become more intimately attuned to this state of "simply being," you may find yourself immersed in the energy of self-discovery. Here, you can commune with your true essence, your higher self, and the wisdom that resides within. Listen attentively, and you may receive profound guidance and inspiration from the depths of your being.

This exploration grants you the ability to traverse the realms of intuition, creativity, and self-awareness with ease and grace. As you traverse this boundless landscape, you will realize the inherent connection between your inner world and the outer reality you experience in waking life.

Through repeated practice of Exercise 6, you will grow in your ability to access Focus 15 effortlessly, unlocking the gateway to the "ALL THAT IS" within you. Trust in your intuitive capacities, for they are the conduits through which you may comprehend the vastness of existence.

Embrace this exploration of Focus 15 with an open heart and an adventurous spirit. Let the timeless nature of this state guide you to deeper self-awareness and a heightened sense of interconnectedness with the universe. As you conclude Wave V, carry the wisdom of Focus 15 with you, for it is a profound tool for self-discovery and transformation in your journey through life.

ENERGY WALKS: EMBARKING ON A JOURNEY OF BOUNDLESS EXPLORATION

As you continue to delve into the realms of Non-Verbal Communication (NVC), a vast world of personal exploration and growth awaits you. With your expanding knowledge and understanding of NVC, you have the power to create countless possibilities for your journey ahead. Here are some suggestions to ignite your imagination and generate your own unique exploration concepts:

Time Travel and Soul Reflection: Take a step back in time and project your consciousness forward into the future. Ask yourself, "Who or what was I before this present life?" and follow it with the inquiry, "Who or what will I become in my next life experience?" Explore the connections between the past, present, and future, contemplating whether the future can influence the past, and vice versa. Visualize yourself growing in the ways you desire, and observe how this newfound awareness impacts your current experiences.

Communicate with Consciousness: Open yourself to communicate with the individual consciousness of all living things. What do you perceive from the energy contained within a cloud? Can you establish a nonverbal communication with a flower? Observe the nonverbal cues and signals a dog uses to interact with its environment.

Embrace the Flow of Life: Sense the movement, vitality, and life forces swirling around and within you, akin to being submerged in the ocean's surf. Feel the ebb and flow of energy within the currents of existence.

Transcend Time and Space: Trust in your NVC abilities as you venture beyond the confines of familiar time, space, and physical matter. Experience being a part of a nonphysical energy system. Explore its unique scenery and connect with potential residents.

Unity with Nature: Visualize reaching out and gently grasping a branch from a tree. Feel its solid connection to both the earth and the sky, allowing the energies from above and below to flow harmoniously within you.

Embrace the Wind's Whispers: Allow a gentle breeze to caress you, recognizing the energy that enables you to move freely, to feel light, to float, to fly, and to harmonize with the universe's rhythm.

Delve into the Depths: Journey to the heart of the earth, exploring the core of existence. Contemplate the experience of going deep within yourself, unraveling the mysteries that lie beneath the surface of your consciousness.

Each of these Energy Walks serves as a portal to unparalleled self-discovery and understanding. As you embark on these explorations, immerse yourself in the wonders of NVC and the expansive possibilities it offers. Trust in your innate abilities, and let your intuition guide you on this extraordinary journey of the self. As you continue to evolve, embrace the interconnectedness of all existence, and be open to the profound insights that await you. Through these Energy Walks, you will uncover the beauty of existence and unlock the depths of your soul's wisdom, enriching your spiritual path and unveiling the boundless potential within you.

What do you think you're experiencing? Consider the experience of going deep within yourself.

What do you think you're experiencing this time?

Wave VI: Odyssey

Welcome to Wave VI: Odyssey, a transformative journey into the boundless realms of human consciousness. Inspired by Robert Monroe's pioneering experiences, this wave will guide you through a profound exploration of your innate abilities and the interconnected nature of existence.

Robert Monroe's OBEs, beginning in 1957, served as a pivotal turning point in his life. These experiences led to the development of the "classic OBE," where one perceives their consciousness as separate from the physical body. However, Bob's journey didn't end there. As he delved deeper into altered states of consciousness, he realized that "outer space" and "inner space" were one and the same. He coined the term "phasing" to describe the process of projecting his consciousness beyond the physical body while maintaining control over a portion of it within.

Phasing is a phenomenon we experience daily without even noticing. Our consciousness can move in and out of various levels of awareness simultaneously. It can traverse time and space, be present in different realities, and even focus on multiple points of existence. This remarkable ability underlies various psychic and paranormal phenomena, from Lucid Dreaming to Near-Death Experiences.

In Wave VI, you will harness the power of phasing to its fullest potential. The exercises in Focus 12, based on Bob's original explorations, will acquaint you with the "second body" or the energy body surrounding your physical form. With practice, you will learn to expand and control this energy body, enabling you to explore far-reaching realms of physical reality.

Throughout your Odyssey, embrace the experiences as they come, knowing that they are precisely what you need at the moment. Express gratitude for the insights you gain during these exercises, acknowledging the assistance provided.

As you progress, Wave VI will take you beyond the limits of your current reality and into other dimensions and states of awareness. Focus 21 will serve as your gateway to expanded consciousness, opening doors to realms beyond our comprehension. Verbal descriptions may fall short in explaining these profound experiences, and each individual's journey will be unique.

Remember, you hold the tools to chart your own course. Bob's wise counsel echoes through time: "Only you have the ability to change." As you give significance and meaning to your experiences, you will foster personal growth and development.

In this wave, you will complete each exercise in sequence, building upon the techniques learned. With practice, you'll be able to repeat the experiences effectively even without explicit instructions. Trust in yourself and your greater capabilities, for they are ever-present to guide and support you.

Embark on your Odyssey with enthusiasm and an open heart, embracing the mysteries of consciousness and unveiling the boundless potential that lies within. Remember, the more you practice, the easier it becomes. Now, let the exploration begin!

Odyssey #1: Sensing

Welcome to Odyssey—Sensing. In this exercise, we will reconnect you with Focus 12 and introduce you to your energy body, also known as the second body. The second body is a dynamic field of energy that surrounds and interconnects with your physical body. Some refer to it as the etheric body, subtle body, or light body, while others liken it to the life force that gives vitality to the physical form. Regardless of the terminology, this energy field is alive, vibrating, and intimately connected to your physical self.

By delving into Exercise 1, you will gain valuable insights into how to control and manipulate your energy body. Focus 12 will serve as the gateway to this exploration, allowing you to experience the presence and influence of your second body.

As you immerse yourself in this exercise, let your consciousness attune to Focus 12, embracing the expanded awareness it offers. Allow yourself to sense and feel the vibrancy of your energy body, acknowledging its seamless connection with your physical form. Through practice and intent, you will learn to navigate and direct this energy, unlocking a whole new dimension of self-awareness and self-mastery.

Stay open to the sensations and revelations that arise during this journey. Embrace the profound nature of your energy body and its potential for transformative experiences. This exercise marks the beginning of your adventure into the depths of your consciousness, so trust in the process and embrace the wonders that await you.

Odyssey #2: Expansion

Welcome to Exercise 2, Expansion. In this exercise, we will take your exploration of the energy body in Focus 12 to the next level by focusing on its expansion. Through a process of increasing the speed of vibrations within your energy body, you will create a profound shift, extending the boundaries of your consciousness outward. This expansion will give rise to the sensation of a vast bubble enveloping your physical form.

As you engage in this exercise, direct your awareness towards your energy body and initiate the process of acceleration. Feel the vibrations quickening, propelling you into an expanded state of being. Gradually, you will perceive the immense bubble that surrounds you, representing the newfound freedom and boundless potential of your energy body.

With your consciousness fully expanded, allow yourself to journey towards the outer reaches of your energy body. As you venture farther from the confines of your physical form, you will experience a lightness and liberation unlike anything you've encountered before.

Trust in the process, and let the feelings of expansion and liberation guide you through this remarkable odyssey. Embrace the vastness of your energy body and the infinite possibilities that lay before you. As you venture further, you may encounter new insights, revelations, and connections with the profound nature of your consciousness.

Remember, practice is the key to mastering this expansion. Each time you embark on this journey, you will refine your ability to traverse the boundless expanse of your energy body with ease and grace. Continue with determination and curiosity, and the exploration of your consciousness will lead you to new horizons of self-discovery.

Odyssey #3: Point of Departure

By now, you have honed your skills in navigating within your expanded energy body, and you are ready for the next phase of this transformative journey. In this exercise, we will guide you to Focus 12 once more, where your consciousness will undergo a fascinating transformation.

As you enter Focus 12, your awareness will shift to your energy body, vibrating at a rapid rate. This time, we will introduce a new technique—rotating your energy body 180 degrees. This rotational movement may feel familiar if you've participated in previous exercises from The Gateway Experience. However, this time, the starting point will be entirely different—your energy body.

As you engage in this rotation, be open to the various sensations and perceptions that arise. Some may describe it as a slow, deliberate journey through time and space, while others may experience a profound shift in awareness—almost as if they have eyes in the back of their heads. Each individual's experience will be unique and personal.

During this process, you may even catch a glimpse of your physical body. But remember, the ultimate goal of Exercise 3 is to project your consciousness out of phase with your physical form as much as possible. It is essential not to set rigid expectations and to remain open to whatever unfolds during this exploration.

If you find this exercise challenging, do not be disheartened. Not everyone will have an out-of-body experience where they are fully aware of their presence. The journey to such states requires practice and patience. Unresolved fears or apprehensions may also play a role in your progress, so be gentle with yourself as you navigate this path of self-discovery.

Avoid putting excessive pressure on yourself to achieve an OBE, as intense effort may become a hindrance. Instead, maintain a nonchalant and relaxed attitude toward the experience. Remember that out-of-body experiences are just one facet of the profound process of self-discovery and personal growth that lies ahead.

With each practice, you are gaining valuable insights into the boundless nature of your consciousness. Embrace the journey with curiosity and an open heart, for there are limitless discoveries waiting to be unveiled. Trust in the process, and you will uncover the wonders that reside within the depths of your being.

Odyssey #4: Nonphysical Friends

The idea of asking for and receiving assistance is something I encourage you to be open to.. The enthusiasm for doing so stems from early encounters with the Explorer sessions, which ignited your curiosity. During these sessions, it became evident that the Explorers were not alone; instead, they had an abundance of assistance. "Helpers in energetic form" would often surround the explorer, standing on either side of them—two on each side. These helpers may aid the explorer in leaving their physical body or contribute in various ways to achieve the session's objectives. Their benevolent intentions were unmistakably clear, even if the specifics of how these nonphysical friends were assisting weren't immediately apparent. Who are these mysterious non-physical companions? We believe it is best for you to make your own assessment.

In Exercise 4, we invite you to establish trust by making direct, personal contact with these nonphysical friends. As you delve into the depths of Focus 12, open your heart and mind to the possibility of connecting with these benevolent beings. Allow your intuition and inner knowing to guide you as you seek their presence.

You may experience their presence in various ways—through feelings, sensations, or even visual impressions. Trust that they are there to support and guide you on your journey of exploration. If you encounter any apprehensions or doubts, remember that these nonphysical friends are here to assist you with love and compassion. They are here to help you expand your consciousness and embrace the wonders of the unseen realms.

As you build a connection with these nonphysical friends, you will come to understand that you are part of a vast, interconnected web of consciousness. Through their guidance and presence, you may gain insights and understanding that go beyond the limitations of your physical senses.

Throughout this exercise, remain open and receptive to the subtle cues and signals that these nonphysical friends may offer. Express your gratitude for their assistance and acknowledge the wisdom they share with you. Know that you are never alone on this journey of exploration; you are supported and surrounded by beings who are eager to assist you on your path of self-discovery.

In the realm of consciousness exploration, there are no limitations to the connections you can forge. Embrace the opportunity to interact with these nonphysical friends, for their presence can profoundly enrich your experiences and understanding.

With each encounter and communication, you will deepen your connection to the broader spectrum of existence. Trust in the process, and allow yourself to be guided by the wisdom of these nonphysical companions.

As you engage in this profound exchange, remember that your intentions and emotions play a significant role in shaping your experiences. Approach this exercise with an open heart and an attitude of gratitude, and you will find that the pathways of communication open even wider.

Enjoy this journey of connecting with your nonphysical friends and know that the bonds you create in these realms transcend time and space. The insights and revelations you receive will be cherished gifts on your continuing odyssey of exploration and self-discovery.

Now, as we embark on this adventure of encountering nonphysical friends, let us remain open to the mysteries and wonders that await us in the realms beyond the physical. Trust in your innate ability to communicate and connect, and you will unveil new dimensions of consciousness that will forever transform the way you perceive reality. Embrace the unknown with courage and curiosity, for it is through these encounters that we expand our understanding of the vast tapestry of existence.

With a heart full of gratitude and excitement, let us continue our journey together, guided by the wisdom and guidance of our nonphysical companions. Let us delve deeper into the realms of consciousness and uncover the limitless possibilities that await us. The voyage continues—onward, to new horizons of exploration.

Odyssey #5: Intro to Focus 21

Odyssey #5 is a transformative exercise that introduces participants to Focus 21—an extraordinary state of awareness known as the bridge to other energy systems. This state was previously exclusive to the institute's residential programs, but now you have the opportunity to explore it from the comfort of your own space.

During this exercise, participants are guided into Focus 21 through specialized Hemi-Sync® signals and verbal guidance. The transition from Focus 12 to Focus 21 involves being attuned to subtle changes in vibrations and feelings of movement within the body.

Focus 21 is a realm of expanded awareness, where conventional notions of time and space become blurred. It serves as a gateway to other energy systems, enabling communication and exploration beyond the limitations of the physical world.

In this state, participants may encounter energies, entities, or aspects of themselves that exist beyond ordinary perception. The experience encourages open-mindedness and receptivity to profound insights and revelations.

Being in Focus 21 allows individuals to explore a broad range of experiences without the constraints of time and space. It is a realm where consciousness transcends limitations and connects with broader aspects of existence.

Participants are encouraged to approach the exploration with gentle curiosity and wonder. Each experience in Focus 21 offers an opportunity for personal growth and understanding.

Navigating this bridge to other energy systems offers an expansion of consciousness and a chance to connect with the vastness of one's inner being. Gratitude is encouraged for the opportunity to delve into the mysteries of consciousness and gain insights into the greater tapestry of existence.

Throughout the exercise, participants are reminded that they are supported by benevolent energies that assist in the journey of self-discovery. The knowledge gained in Focus 21 enriches one's path of growth and self-realization.

In summary, Odyssey #5 provides participants with an informative and transformative experience of Focus 21—a state of expanded awareness and a bridge to other energy systems. Through gentle exploration, individuals can deepen their understanding of consciousness and connect with the infinite possibilities of existence.

Odyssey #6: Free Flow Focus 21

Focus 21 offers a unique and transformative experience, combining the culmination of your previous efforts with the exploration of uncharted territory. Throughout this exercise, it is essential to maintain focus and heightened awareness.

The process begins by projecting your consciousness and guidance directly into the light of Focus 21, effortlessly transitioning from Focus 12. This seamless journey allows you to access the elevated state of awareness that Focus 21 offers.

Once in Focus 21, you are encouraged to seek assistance and guidance from entities whose wisdom, development, and experiences surpass or equal your own. These beings are present within this realm, offering their support and insights to aid you in your explorations.

The beauty of this exercise lies in its boundless potential. There are no limitations to the number of times you can participate in this free flow journey, and each experience holds the promise of rich and abundant rewards. The possibilities for discovery and growth are endless, waiting to be unveiled during your time in Focus 21.

As you engage in this exercise, remain open to the various encounters and revelations that may arise. Embrace the freedom of exploration and the vastness of the unknown, allowing your consciousness to roam in this state of expanded awareness.

This exercise serves as a profound opportunity for self-discovery and connection with higher consciousness. With each journey into Focus 21, you have the chance to deepen your understanding, broaden your horizons, and embark on a journey of endless transformation.

Approach this exercise with enthusiasm and an open heart, for the potential for growth and enlightenment is limitless. Trust in your innate abilities and the guidance available to you in Focus 21, and let your consciousness flow freely in this realm of boundless possibilities.

Wave VII: Voyager

Wave VII: Voyager is dedicated to the exploration of deep states of awareness associated with the afterlife realm. The main purpose here is to be of service to yourself and others. As you enter and operate within Focus 23 through Focus 27, you will encounter individuals who have passed away physically but have remained connected to the earthly energy systems, known as "static" entities. The primary objective is to provide assistance to these souls, guiding them to move beyond the earthly experience and transition to a designated "reception center" at Focus 27. Here, they can rest, review their life experiences, and contemplate their next steps in their evolutionary journey.

Guided by your Inner Helper, you will initially explore your complete self in Focus 21. This essential groundwork will prepare you for operating at higher levels of concentration in future exercises. Embrace the understanding that your experiences are precisely what you need at this moment in time, and expressing heartfelt gratitude for any assistance received is encouraged.

Throughout these exercises, have faith in yourself and acknowledge that a greater aspect of your being is always available to assist and guide you. Completing each exercise in sequence is vital as they build upon the tools and techniques learned in the previous stages. Regular practice will enhance your ability to repeat and navigate the experiences effectively, even without explicit instructions.

To overcome limiting beliefs, allow your intentions and willingness to explore to be your guiding principles. Embrace the realization that you are more than just your physical body, and the journey of self-discovery and personal growth continues to unfold. Keeping a journal of your explorations is highly recommended, as it can aid in reflecting upon and comprehending the profound insights gained throughout The Gateway Experience.

Your dedication to personal development is greatly appreciated, and we extend our heartfelt gratitude for your ongoing support. As you delve into the depths of consciousness and expand your understanding of the afterlife realm, may this transformative journey be one of profound learning and enlightenment. Trust in the process, and let the voyage into the unknown realms of consciousness be a remarkable and enlightening experience.

Voyager #1: Explore Total Self

The primary objective is to delve deeper into the understanding of your entire self. With the guidance of your Inner Helper, you will embark on a journey to uncover the purpose behind your physical existence. Your Inner Helper, your closest friend and ally, possesses a profound knowledge and understanding of you, surpassing your conscious awareness.

This exploration will take place within Focus 21, a state of consciousness that serves as a bridge between different reality systems. From this vantage point, you will establish a powerful communication channel with your Inner Helper. Through this connection, you will have the opportunity to pose a series of questions, gaining valuable insights and information about the nature and significance of your earthly life.

Allow yourself to be open and receptive to the guidance that comes forth during this exploration. Embrace the wisdom and understanding offered by your Inner Helper as you uncover the deeper meaning behind your existence. Trust in the process, and with the assistance of your trusted guide, venture into the realms of self-discovery and enlightenment.

Voyager #2: Intro to Focus 23

Focus 23, you will embark on your first conscious experience in the transitional reality of Focus 23. This realm is inhabited by individuals who have recently completed their physical life but find themselves unable to move on for various reasons. The techniques you have learned will guide you as you proceed to Focus 21, and during this exercise, special Hemi-Sync® signals and verbal guidance will accompany you as you relax into this state of awareness. Pay close attention to the subtle changes in vibrations or sensations of movement in your body as you transition through the different states of consciousness, according to your choosing.

Upon entering Focus 23, your task will be to observe and perceive the various beings and their states of consciousness. You may encounter individuals who display emotions such as bewilderment, shock, and confusion due to their current condition. It's essential to remember that you are always in complete control of your experience, and you will maintain your composure and confidence throughout.

Take this opportunity to gather knowledge about everything you see, as it serves as a starting point for the assistance you can offer to many. However, for now, you will only be acting as an observer and will not engage with any of these beings. In the event that someone approaches you, simply offer them love and request their guides to provide assistance. Exercise 5 will provide you with the chance to return to this area and extend your help to the team members present.

Voyager #3: Intro to Focus 25

You will explore Focus 25, known as the belief system territory. This region is inhabited by groups of nonphysical humans who have settled here over thousands of years, embracing and adhering to various premises and concepts during their existence.

In this exercise, you will be verbally guided to Focus 25, with an initial stop in Focus 23, which serves as a transition point. It's essential to note that Focus 25 contains all the world's religious beliefs, and your role is that of an observer. You are not to actively participate but simply observe and take in the experiences and memories during your time here.

As you traverse this realm, you may encounter individuals you are familiar with; however, always remember that you are merely a visitor, tasked with observation and understanding. The belief systems you encounter are tools used in constructing reality, allowing individuals to shape and perceive their experiences within certain boundaries while expanding other aspects.

Throughout this exercise, maintain a non-participatory stance and embrace the role of an observer. Your insights and memories from this journey will serve to enrich your understanding of the diverse beliefs that shape the human experience in the afterlife.

Voyager #4: Intro to Focus 27

A transitional space between physical and virtual existences. This area serves as a way station, providing a comforting and familiar setting for relaxation, meeting others, seeking assistance, and engaging in communication and consultation.

The primary purpose of Focus 27 is to ease the transition for those who have just departed from their physical environments. It serves as a supportive environment, alleviating any trauma or shock associated with the afterlife experience. Here, newly arrived individuals can find calmness and rationality with the guidance of counselors.

As visitors to this place, you are still connected to the realm of physical matter reality. Keep in mind that Focus 27 is vast, and you should be open to perceiving beyond just visuals. Sensations, feelings, impressions, and knowing are equally valuable modes of perception in this space.

During your exploration, allow yourself to discover or create a special place that resonates with you. This place will serve as a meeting point where you can reconnect with friends and loved ones during your regular sleep cycle. It's a space to nurture relationships and connections beyond physical boundaries.

In Exercise 5, you will return to Focus 27 with a specific purpose: to assist those who may be stuck in

Focus 23. Your role as a helper in this realm holds significant potential for aiding others in their journey of transition and growth. Trust your intuition and embrace this opportunity to be of service to those in need.

Voyager #5: Retrieval

The primary objective of this exercise is to equip you with the skills to offer assistance to individuals in Focus 23. Before proceeding, it is essential to temporarily set aside any skeptical, critical, or analytical thoughts, allowing yourself to be fully present and open to experiencing the moment. Be receptive to various forms of perception and communication beyond the traditional five senses.

As you transition to Focus 27, you will seek guidance and support for a "rescue run." Special Hemi-Sync® signals and verbal instructions will facilitate your relaxation and entry into Focus 27. Pay close attention to subtle changes in vibrations or feelings of movement as you traverse the different states of consciousness.

In Focus 27, you will encounter beings who have recently completed their physical lives but are unable to move on for various reasons. Your role is to observe and perceive without direct interaction, maintaining your composure and confidence in this new environment.

Focus 27 is a region that contains the belief system territory, where various groups of nonphysical humans have settled over thousands of years, adhering to diverse premises and concepts.

As you explore Focus 27, remember that your purpose is to observe and take in the information. Avoid engaging with the beings you encounter, as you are a visitor to this realm, gaining insights and experiences without direct involvement.

During this exercise, you may encounter familiar faces, but it's crucial to maintain your role as an observer and gather information to assist others later.

Beliefs in Focus 27 serve as tools to construct reality, shaping different aspects of existence. As you witness the diversity of beliefs, remain open-minded and receptive to perceptions beyond visual cues, such as feelings, impressions, knowing, and more.

Throughout this experience, be attentive to subtle sensations, which may include:

- A "lightening" effect in the energy around you.

- Sudden changes in your core body temperature, feeling warmer or cooler.

- Vibrant bursts of color.

- An increase in heart rate.

- A general feeling of energy surging through your body.

- Tingling sensations in your hands, arms, or feet.

- A cool breeze or fluttering sensations on your face or hands.

- Goosebumps or chills on your neck or arms.

Remember that regardless of whether you perceive such sensations, proceed with the assumption that guidance is present with you, as you have learned from previous experiences.

After observing and gathering insights, you will have the opportunity to create a special place within Focus 27, a meeting point to return to during your regular sleep cycle. This space will allow you to connect with friends and those you care about, even if they are currently in Focus 23.

Exercise 5 will also prepare you to return to Focus 23 in the future to offer assistance to those who are stuck there. Trust in the process and allow your experiences to unfold naturally as you develop and refine your skills as a Voyager.

Upon completion of the exercise, you will gradually return through the various levels of consciousness to full waking consciousness. You are encouraged to use this exercise repeatedly, aiding those in Focus 23 and advancing your understanding and abilities as a Voyager.

Voyager #6: Messages from Beyond

The final exercise in the Voyager series is distinct from the previous ones as it follows a more open and unstructured format. There is no formal preparation process, and there won't be a count-up or count-down. Instead, using the Hemi-Sync® frequencies, you will enter the Focus 27 state, enabling communication with your loved ones and other benevolent beings.

In this free-flowing exercise, you have the opportunity to connect with individuals of your choice and send messages to them. While there will be limited verbal guidance, you will be guided to Focus 27, where you can establish communication with those you wish to interact with.

Take this opportunity to express your thoughts, feelings, and love to your dear ones on the other side, or simply be receptive to any messages they may have for you. In Focus 27, you can connect with loving beings and engage in meaningful exchanges.

Embrace this unique experience with an open heart and an open mind, for it may provide profound insights and healing. Enjoy this special connection with those beyond the physical realm and explore the boundless possibilities of communication in this heightened state of awareness.

As you conclude this final exercise of the Voyager series, take time to reflect on your journey as an Explorer. Your experiences, growth, and understanding of consciousness have expanded in ways beyond imagination. The Gateway Experience has been a transformative voyage, enabling you to explore the vast realms of human consciousness.

We extend our gratitude for your dedication to personal growth and exploration. Carry the knowledge and insights gained from this program into your daily life, embracing the essence of self-discovery and connection to the greater universe.

With the Gateway Experience complete, you are now equipped to continue your journey of self-discovery, expansion, and inner exploration beyond these audio exercises. Trust in the infinite possibilities that reside within you and embrace the incredible journey of consciousness that lies ahead.

As you return to full waking consciousness, remember that you can revisit any of these exercises whenever you desire, further enriching your connection to the realms of consciousness explored throughout the Voyager series. Thank you for your commitment and participation in The Gateway Experience.

Encoding Instructions

Incorporating Encoding into the program can enhance your overall experience and amplify the desired outcomes. Encoding involves establishing specific triggers or signals that elicit certain responses or occurrences within your consciousness. As you engage in the tape exercises, you'll create mental triggers, represented by thought patterns, that signify your desired outcomes.

To make these encodings more effective, you can pair them with specific physical actions like breaths or hand movements. This combination helps reinforce the mental triggers and facilitates a deeper interaction with different levels of consciousness. The repeated use of these encodings in C-1 (physical reality) strengthens their potency, making them more powerful tools for your exploration.

To become physically wide awake and alert, you can try the following encoding: Touch the back of your neck with the fingers of your right hand while mentally repeating the number one several times. This simple action helps heighten your senses and prepares you for a more focused and alert state (Discovery #2).

To boost your energy levels during the Threshold (#4) and Freedom (#5) phases, you can use another encoding technique: Close your physical eyes and extend your hands outward with palms facing up, as if receiving fresh energy. Take a moment to visualize pure, white energy flowing from above, entering your palms, traveling through your arms, and permeating your entire being. Inhale deeply, holding your breath momentarily, and feel the revitalizing effects of this energy infusion. Finally, take a deep breath, open your eyes, and feel the renewed sense of energy within you.

By incorporating encodings and triggers into your Gateway Experience, you can deepen your connection with your consciousness, enhance your focus, and achieve more profound insights and results. These techniques can be customized to suit your preferences and intentions, making your journey of self-discovery even more enriching and rewarding. Embrace the power of encoding as you continue to explore the limitless realms of your consciousness.

FOCUS 10 (DISCOVERY #3, THRESHOLD #5):

Focus 10 is a state where your mind remains alert while your body enters a deep state of relaxation and sleep. To enter Focus 10, you initiate a mental trigger by breathing in sparkling energy, saying or thinking the number ten, and then exhaling. This process creates a bridge between wakefulness and relaxation, allowing you to maintain awareness while your body achieves a deep state of rest.

FOCUS 12 (THRESHOLD #1):

Moving from Focus 10 to Focus 12 marks a significant shift in your awareness, as you enter an expanded state of consciousness. The transition is simple—just count from ten to twelve. In Focus 12, you'll experience heightened intuition, profound insights, and a deeper connection with your inner self.

HEALING (THRESHOLD #4):

In this technique, you tap into the power of visualization and intention to promote healing within your physical body. By closing your eyes and taking a deep breath, you initiate the process of restoring balance and health. Visualize the soothing color purple, and direct this healing energy to the part of your body that requires assistance. Repeating "Heal, balance" in your mind reinforces the intention for optimal results.

MEMORY (DISCOVERY #2, THRESHOLD #5, FREEDOM #2):

Memory enhancement involves accessing past experiences and information more effectively. To set a pattern for improved memory, enter Focus 12 and create a detailed mental model of the situation or memory you want to recall. Then, with a powerful and certain intent, send this model out into your expanded awareness. This encoding facilitates improved recall and retrieval of memories when needed.

PHYSICAL STRENGTH AND AGILITY:

This technique empowers you to enhance your physical abilities beyond your usual limits. By focusing on the physical act you want to perform and envisioning the vibrant color energy of red, you stimulate a surge of energy and strength, enabling you to excel in the desired physical activity.

PROBLEM SOLVING (THRESHOLD #2):

To receive insightful answers and solutions to problems, start by taking a deep breath and drawing fresh energy into your physical head. As you exhale, think of the number twelve, symbolizing higher consciousness, and then pose your question or present the issue at hand. Trust that the answers will come, and be open to receiving them in various forms.

RELAX (THRESHOLD #6):

Stress reduction and relaxation are crucial for overall well-being. By visualizing the number ten and taking a deep breath in, you initiate the process of relaxation. As you exhale slowly, imagine all harmful tension and emotions leaving your mind and body. This encoding helps you find calm and peace within yourself.

REBAL (RE-ENTER BALANCE):

The REBAL technique allows you to reabsorb a special energy pattern you've created during the exercises. Inhale and envision a moving circle with the number 10 inside it as your REBAL. By letting the circle move around you, you effortlessly reabsorb this energy pattern, promoting balance and harmony within your being.

RETURN TO C-1 (DISCOVERY #3):

When it's time to return to full waking consciousness after an exercise, think of the number one while moving the fingers of your right hand. This encoding serves as a gentle and effective way to bring your awareness back to the present moment.

SLEEP (DISCOVERY #5):

Achieving restful sleep is essential for rejuvenation and overall health. To fall asleep naturally and peacefully, mentally count slowly from one to twenty. When you reach twenty, your mind will be in a normal, restful state of sleep, facilitating deep and refreshing rest.

STRESS REDUCTION (THRESHOLD #4):

Stress is a common challenge, and this technique helps release emotional pressure and tension. Close your eyes, take a deep breath, and envision the calming energy of the color green. Exhale, allowing all excess and harmful emotional charges to flow downward and out through the soles of your feet, promoting emotional equilibrium.

Each of these techniques and encodings can be combined or used individually to tailor your Gateway Experience to your unique needs and goals. As you become more adept at incorporating these practices into your life, you'll unlock the profound potential of your consciousness and experience transformational growth. Enjoy your continued journey of self-discovery and exploration through The Gateway Experience!

Trouble Shooting

During The Gateway Process, participants may encounter various challenges and questions. The Monroe Institute has compiled a list of some of the most encountered issues based on their extensive experience with the program. They have diligently worked to understand and resolve these challenges to support participants on their transformative journeys. However, it's essential to acknowledge that less common issues may arise as well. In such instances, adopting a problem-solving approach can be beneficial, empowering you to explore potential solutions independently. The following section provides guidance on addressing these issues and finding resolutions to ensure a fulfilling and successful experience. It is important to note here that these are questions and answers from the institute, re-written in this summary. They do not represent my personal thoughts or experiences with the tapes.

Q: In the case of various images or dream-like thoughts interfering with what I'm trying to do on a tape, what should I do?

A: When encountering images or dream-like thoughts during your session, avoid suppressing or forcefully pushing them away. Instead, practice gentle acknowledgement without becoming too engaged with them, as this may lead to drowsiness or distraction. Take a brief moment to observe these images, then allow them to naturally dissipate. Remember, you can always return to explore them at a later time, but for now, maintain your focus on the intended exercise. Trust that your subconscious mind will retain these experiences for future exploration if needed.

Q: I'm unable or unwilling to vocalize when using the Resonant Tuning technique. My body enters a deep state of relaxation, and my mouth doesn't seem to want to cooperate. What should I do? I either sing along in my head, click out, or go into some sort of thought dream: What should I do?

A: Engaging in Resonant Tuning requires discipline as it is a valuable method to perceive and control nonphysical energy. While practicing Resonant Tuning, try to persist in vocalizing even if it feels uncomfortable initially. This technique helps gather your vibrational energy and reduces internal dialogue, ultimately enhancing your experiences with the audios. As you continue to use this method, the discomfort associated with vocalization is likely to diminish. If you find yourself mentally singing or wandering into thought dreams, gently redirect your focus back to vocalization, ensuring an active participation in the process. Your commitment to the practice will lead to improved results and a deeper connection with nonphysical realms.

Q: When I listen to the audios, I notice a buzzing or pressure in my forehead, as well as an acceleration of my heartbeat. What's all this? Is this a normal occurrence?

A: Yes, experiencing a light buzzing or pressure sensation in your forehead is a common occurrence for some individuals during the Hemi-Sync® process. These sensations indicate that you are reacting to the audio in a significant way. However, if you are feeling a great deal of discomfort, it's possible that the volume of the audio is too high. Adjust the volume to a level where you can comfortably hear the verbal instructions for the best results.

It's important to remember that as you expand your state of awareness with the audios, you become more attuned to bodily functions like heartbeat and breathing. These physiological changes are a natural part of energy level transitions, such as moving from Consciousness 1 to Focus 10. Embrace these sensations as signs of your heightened awareness and allow yourself to fully immerse in the transformative journey of The Gateway Experience.

Q: My high energy states don't appear to be present, and I am having difficulty visualizing what they should feel like.

A: It's important to understand that high energy states can manifest differently for each individual. Not everyone will experience them in the same way. Some people may see light, colors, or forms, while others may feel sensations such as tingling or shaking in their body, bed, or surroundings. Additionally, some individuals may hear rushing sounds, buzzing, voices, verbal messages, or even music during these states.

If you are having difficulty visualizing or feeling these high energy states, remember that there is no specific right or wrong way to perceive them. Relax and remain open to your unique perceptions without forcing any specific feelings or experiences. Allow yourself to be present in the moment and observe any subtle changes or sensations that may arise.

Each journey through The Gateway Experience is personal and distinct, and your experiences are valid and meaningful, regardless of how they manifest. Trust in the process, and know that your exploration of consciousness will unfold in its own unique way. Embrace the journey with an open heart and a curious mind, and you will continue to uncover the wonders of your consciousness.

Q: I'm having trouble staying awake while doing the taped exercises. What options do I have in this situation?

A: If you find it challenging to stay awake during the taped exercises, there are several steps you can take to enhance your alertness. Firstly, ensure you are well-rested before starting the exercise. Being in a state of adequate rest can help you maintain focus and attention during the session.

Secondly, consider incorporating some light stretches or movement before beginning the exercise. This can help awaken your body and mind, making it easier to stay alert.

Thirdly, use the concept of sleep as an energy conversion tool. Mentally put the idea of sleep into an "Energy Conversion Box," allowing your mind to focus on staying awake and engaged.

If you still struggle to stay awake, try changing your physical position. For example, consider sitting up during the exercise instead of lying down. This change in posture may help you remain more alert.

Lastly, remember that practice and patience are key. The ability to strike the right balance between deep relaxation and wakefulness may require time and consistent effort. Don't be discouraged if it takes time to find the optimal state for your exploration.

Incorporate these strategies, and over time, you will likely find it easier to stay awake and fully engaged during the taped exercises, enhancing your overall experience and deepening your journey of self-discovery.

Q: I'm having trouble forming and maintaining control over my EBT. Sometimes it appears to be a triangle or an extension of my own arm, depending on the situation. Is this a normal occurrence?

A: Yes, it is entirely normal for the EBT (Energy Balloon Tool) to take different forms or shapes depending on your current state of mind and intention. The EBT is a versatile tool that can adapt to your needs and the specific task at hand. Each time you use it, there is no need for it to be the same as before; it can change forms while you are using it.

The primary purpose of the EBT is to concentrate and direct nonphysical energy. Its applications are vast, from healing (Threshold #G: LBM) to perceiving distant events and people (Freedom #2: Remote Viewing) or entering other energy systems (Threshold #5: EBT). It can assist you in various aspects of exploration and self-discovery.

Embrace the fluidity and adaptability of the EBT. Trust your intuition and imagination in shaping it to suit your needs in different situations. With practice and intention, you will find that your control over the EBT becomes more refined and effective, unlocking new dimensions of your consciousness and expanding your abilities in the Gateway Experience. Remember, the power lies within you and your willingness to explore the endless possibilities that the EBT offers.

Q: Occasionally, while listening to a tape, I feel so much energy in my body that it becomes uncomfortable, and I want to get out of the tape as soon as possible. What should I do in this situation?

A: It's essential to recognize that the discomfort you feel is a natural part of the process as you tap into second-state energy – nonphysical energy that is essential for your expanded awareness and consciousness. Embrace the experience as a sign of progress on your journey of exploration and self-discovery.

To alleviate any discomfort, take control of the energy flow within your body. You can do this by consciously directing the energy and observing its movement throughout your entire being. Experiment with speeding up or slowing down the energy flow, finding a pace that feels more comfortable to you.

Remember that this energy is a vital aspect of your practice, and it is through this connection with nonphysical energy that you can achieve higher states of awareness. Embrace the sensation and allow yourself to adapt and grow as you continue your practice of the Gateway Experience.

If at any point you feel overwhelmed, take a moment to breathe deeply and ground yourself. Trust that you are in control of your experience, and by working with the energy consciously, you will gain a deeper understanding of yourself and the boundless potential within you. Keep an open mind and heart, and let the energy guide you on this transformative journey.

Q: Normally, I prefer to sleep on my side or stomach, but I'm uncomfortable sprawled out on my back. In addition, I am unable to remain on my back for an extended period of time without becoming restless. What should I do in this situation?

A: It's completely understandable to have preferences for sleeping positions, and you don't need to force yourself into an uncomfortable position during the audios. Fortunately, there are alternative ways to listen to the tapes and still benefit from the experience.

One option is to try sitting up straight in a comfortable chair or on your bed while listening to the audios. Sitting can help you stay more alert and engaged during the sessions, reducing the likelihood of drifting off to sleep.

If you have a good pair of "ear-bud" headphones, you might be able to find a comfortable position on your side or stomach and still listen to the tapes effectively. Arrange some pillows to support your body while wearing the ear-buds, allowing you to "ride the Waves" in a position that feels more natural to you.

Keep in mind that the important thing is to be relaxed and open to the experience, regardless of your physical position. Find what works best for you and allows you to stay engaged in the Gateway Experience. With some experimentation, you'll discover a setup that suits your comfort and enables you to fully embrace the transformative journey of self-discovery.

Q: I'm conscious of my breathing even when I'm not using Focus 10. This makes it impossible for me to detach myself from the situation or to perceive the high energy states in any other way. Do you have any recommendations?

A: It's not uncommon to be aware of your breathing, even during the Gateway Experience. In fact, this awareness can be used positively to enhance your overall experience. Breathing is a vital aspect of energy charging, as demonstrated in the Resonant Tuning exercises, where you use breath to gather and control nonphysical energy.

Instead of trying to suppress or fight this awareness, embrace it as a natural part of your journey. Allow yourself to be mindful of your breathing while engaging in the exercises on the tapes. Recognize that breathing is a normal bodily function and not a hindrance to your experience. If you find that your awareness of breathing is becoming a major source of concern, you can put this concern into your Energy Conversion Box to set it aside temporarily.

Over time, as you grow more comfortable with the Gateway Experience and the various states of consciousness, the awareness of your breathing should naturally fade into the background. For some individuals, being conscious of breathing or heartbeat serves as a comforting link to physical reality, allowing them to transition more confidently into other states of consciousness after experiencing physical reality.

Remember, each person's journey is unique, and being mindful of your breathing can be an asset rather than a hindrance. Embrace this aspect of your experience and allow it to guide you on your path of self-discovery and exploration.

Q: I had a peak experience during the "Focus 12 Free Flow" session. I'd like to have this experience again. How can I do that?

A: It's wonderful that you had a peak experience during the "Focus 12 Free Flow" session! These moments of heightened awareness and connection are indeed special and unique. However, it's important to approach them with an open mind and avoid trying to recreate or force such experiences to happen again.

Peak experiences are often spontaneous and deeply personal, arising from a combination of factors such as your state of mind, emotional receptivity, and the specific circumstances at that moment. Instead of chasing after a specific peak experience, embrace the concept of continuous discovery and exploration within the Gateway Experience.

Each session and exercise is an opportunity for new insights and growth. Approach each session with a sense of curiosity and openness, allowing yourself to be present in the moment without expectations. By being receptive to whatever unfolds, you may find that new and meaningful experiences naturally emerge.

Treasure the peak experience you had, and remember that every exploration is a valuable step on your journey of self-discovery. The Gateway Experience is not about making these experiences ordinary but rather embracing their uniqueness and using them as stepping stones to deeper understanding and expansion of consciousness in a variety of settings.

Q: I have not been able to visualize my REBAL energy emanating from my head and bending around to reach my feet so far. I'm at a loss.

A: Visualizing the REBAL energy as described can be challenging for some individuals, and that's completely normal. It's important to recognize that visualization is just one mode of perception, and not everyone experiences it in the same way. If you find it difficult to visualize the REBAL, there are alternative ways to work with and perceive this energy.

Instead of focusing solely on visualizing the REBAL, try to sense or feel the energy within and around you. Imagine yourself surrounded and filled with vibrant, sparkling bursts of energy, tingling and radiating throughout your entire being. You can also practice "popping" your REBAL regularly without using the audios, as this can strengthen your connection to the energy.

Remember that the REBAL is a valuable tool for energy work and self-awareness, regardless of how you perceive it. Trust that you are still benefiting from the practice, even if you don't visualize it in the traditional sense. Detailed instructions for working with the REBAL can be found on page 25 in Discovery #3: Advanced Focus 10, providing further insights and techniques for utilizing this energy effectively.

Q: Nonverbal Communication is something that I would like to learn more about (NVC). I believe I'm starting to grasp the concept, but at first I was a little frustrated.

A: Your frustration is completely understandable, as Nonverbal Communication (NVC) can be quite different from traditional verbal communication. NVC operates on a more intuitive and right-brain level, which can be a shift for those of us who are more accustomed to linear and verbal thinking.

NVC is a holistic approach to communication that goes beyond words and focuses more on feelings, impressions, and intuition. It allows us to understand and convey information through nonverbal cues, such as body language, facial expressions, and energetic signals. These forms of communication can often convey emotions and thoughts that words alone cannot express.

For example, consider a beautiful sunset. While words can describe the colors and scenery, they may fall short in capturing the profound emotions it evokes in the observer. NVC allows us to instantly comprehend

Desiree M. Palmer

the entire experience, encompassing both the physical and nonphysical aspects.

As you continue to explore NVC, it's essential to be patient with yourself and allow your intuitive and right-brain functions to develop. Embrace the process of learning and understanding beyond words, and with practice, you'll discover the depth and richness of communication that NVC offers. Remember that NVC provides a unique perspective that complements verbal communication and allows for a more profound connection with others and the world around us.

Q: Using the audios, I've discovered some interesting things, but I'd be even happier if I knew I was getting exactly what the creators intended.

A: It's completely natural to seek validation and confirmation that you are on the right track with the audios. However, it's essential to understand that The Gateway Experience is designed to be a highly individualized and personal journey. Each person's experiences with the audios will be unique and may vary widely.

The creators of The Gateway Experience at The Monroe Institute recognize and embrace the diversity of experiences reported by participants. They understand that no two individuals will have the same journey, and this is precisely the beauty of the program. The audios are intentionally designed to be open-ended, allowing for personal exploration and discovery.

While there may be some common themes and experiences shared by others, it's crucial to focus on the significance and meaning that these experiences hold for you personally. Your unique journey is a reflection of your individual consciousness and growth.

Instead of seeking to match exactly what others have experienced or what the creators intended, embrace the authenticity of your own experiences. Your journey is valid, and the insights and discoveries you make are valuable and meaningful to your personal development.

Remember, The Gateway Experience is about self-discovery, expansion of consciousness, and exploring new realms of awareness. Trust in your own journey, and know that every experience you have is a valuable part of your personal evolution. Embrace the mystery and wonder of your unique exploration with the audios.

Q: While listening to your audios, I was overcome by a dazzling flash of light. Is this light a manifestation of God?

A: Experiencing a dazzling flash of light while listening to the audios is a common phenomenon reported by many individuals during higher states of consciousness and exploration. While some people may interpret this light as a manifestation of God or a divine presence based on their religious beliefs, The Monroe Institute does not endorse any particular religious interpretation or belief system.

The light experience is more likely a reflection of your own heightened state of awareness and expanded consciousness rather than a specific external manifestation. It is a profound experience that can evoke feelings of euphoria, oneness with the universe, and a sense of love and interconnectedness.

In the realm of consciousness exploration, individuals from various cultural and religious backgrounds may have different interpretations of such experiences. In Buddhism, for example, a practitioner might perceive it as a connection with Buddha, while in Islam, it might be seen as a connection with Allah or Mohammed, and in Christianity, it could be interpreted as the light of Christ.

Regardless of religious affiliations, experiencing such a light can be a powerful indication of your spiritual and personal growth, as well as your exploration of nonphysical levels of consciousness. The audios serve as tools for self-discovery and expansion of awareness, allowing you to delve into the depths of your consciousness and explore profound states of being.

Ultimately, the interpretation of your experiences is a deeply personal matter, and it's essential to approach them with an open mind and heart, free from any preconceived notions or expectations. Embrace the wonder and mystery of these experiences as you continue your journey of exploration with the audios.

Q: How many times should I repeat the process with each tape before moving on to the next?

A: The number of times you should repeat each tape before moving on to the next can vary depending on the individual. It is essential to become familiar with and comfortable with the previous tape before progressing, but you do not need to be an expert in it. Some people may find it beneficial to repeat a tape several times to reinforce their understanding and experiences, while others may feel ready to move on after one or two repetitions. The key is to feel confident in your abilities and experiences before moving forward. If you encounter difficulties, don't hesitate to practice or revisit previous tapes for reinforcement. Remember, the journey is unique for each individual, and there is no strict rule on how many times to repeat a tape before progressing. Trust your intuition and pace yourself accordingly.

Q: Are my children allowed to listen to the audios?

A: Yes, using Gateway Experience audios with children can be highly beneficial. Many parents have found it valuable to involve their children in the exploration. However, it is essential for parents to collaborate with their children and be mindful of their progress and experiences. As with any personal development program, parental discretion is crucial. Parents can decide whether or not to share the audios with their children's siblings based on their judgment of each child's readiness and interest in the material. Ultimately, involving children in the journey can be a rewarding and enriching experience, but it should be done with thoughtful consideration and guidance.

Q: I understand that after a while, we don't really need the audios to achieve different states of consciousness. What is the best way to remember the Hemi-Sync® signals?

A: As you progress in your exploration, you will find that you no longer rely on the taped exercises to achieve different states of consciousness. After completing an exercise, it becomes important to remember the sensations and experiences you had during your most effective responses in the desired state of consciousness. A simple deep breath and the act of recalling that state can trigger a shift in consciousness. This technique of recalling and revisiting states becomes more effective with practice. One helpful method is the "One-Breath Technique," described on page 47, which can assist you in quickly accessing desired states of consciousness with just a single breath. Repeated practice will make this process more natural and efficient for you.

Q: Have people reported obtaining worthwhile results from the use of marijuana or other drugs in conjunction with the audios?

A: Some individuals have reported using mind-altering drugs while listening to the audios. The outcomes they've experienced have varied, with some claiming that drugs enhanced their experiences, while others found no significant impact. However, it's essential to emphasize that we strongly advise against the use of illegal drugs. The Gateway Experience is designed to be effective on its own, and adding drugs to the equation may have unpredictable and potentially harmful effects. It's best to explore the program without the use of any substances for the most reliable and safe results.

Q: I have heard that the Hemi-Sync and Gateway process may be dangerous to do as it is the same way they train the participants in MK Ultra and you can lose control of your own mind. Is there any truth to the fact that the same person who created the program also was involved in MK Ultra?

A: The Hemi-Sync technology was developed by Robert A. Monroe, who founded The Monroe Institute in the 1970s. There is no evidence definitively linking him to MK Ultra or any harmful mind-control experiments.

Congratulations!

You've reached the end of The Gateway Experience, but in truth, this journey knows no final destination. It's an adventure of never-ending personal growth, an unfolding path of continuous discovery. So, let's not use the word "completed" because there's always more to explore!

With The Gateway Experience, there are no limitations on how far you can go or how much you can benefit. It's a boundless system, offering you the freedom to develop and evolve your skills whenever you desire. The beauty lies in the fact that each exercise and wave builds upon the last, creating a cumulative effect that keeps pushing you forward.

Throughout this transformative program, you have traveled through seven waves, each guiding you to different states of awareness and unlocking profound insights into the nature of consciousness. From the foundational Discovery in Wave I to the profound Voyager journey in Wave VII, you have embraced the richness of human consciousness and expanded your understanding of the self.

Wave I, allowed you to establish a solid foundation in the art of exploring expanded states of consciousness. You honed your abilities and prepared yourself for the transformative experiences that lay ahead.

Wave II, the "Threshold," took you on a journey through time and space, guiding you to different realms and dimensions, fostering an understanding of the interconnectedness of all things.

In Wave III, "Freedom," you liberated yourself from the constraints of the physical body, exploring alternate realities and encountering profound insights into the true nature of existence.

Wave IV, "Adventure," invited you to explore the depths of your being, facing your fears, and embracing the unlimited potential of your consciousness.

Wave V, "Exploring," allowed you to delve into states of creation and manifestation, harnessing the power of intention and exploring the vast reaches of your consciousness.

Wave VI, "Odyssey," took you on a journey through outer and inner spaces, guiding you to the realization that consciousness knows no bounds.

Now, with Wave VII, "Voyager," you transcend the boundaries of physical existence, reaching out to assist others and exploring the transitional realities of those who have completed their physical life.

As you delve deeper into this program, you'll find that the possibilities for self-discovery are endless. Your dedication to exploration will lead you to new realms of awareness and understanding, unveiling exciting dimensions of your consciousness on a regular basis.

So, keep embracing the journey of self-discovery and let The Gateway Experience be your guiding light. Remember, there's always more to explore, more to learn, and more to discover. This is just the beginning of an incredible adventure that knows no bounds.

I'd love to hear about your unique experience with The Gateway Process! Feel free to get in touch with me through DesireeMPalmer.com.

Also, don't forget to subscribe to my Amazon author page to be the first to know about my new releases. I write a wide range of books, including fiction, nonfiction, and delightful picture books for children. If you ever want to collaborate, I'm always open to exciting projects.

And if you're feeling inspired to embark on your own writing journey, I am happy to help.

Thank you for joining me in this incredible adventure. Remember, there's always more to explore, more to learn, and more to discover. So, keep embracing the journey of self-discovery and let the Gateway Experience be your guiding light. Happy exploring!

Sources
As Listed in the Original CIA Document

Bentov, Itzhak. *Stalking the Wild Pendulum.* New York, E. P. Dutton, 1977.

Ferguson, Marilyn. *"Karl Pribram's Changing Reality"* Human Behavior, May 1978.

Gliedman, John. *"Einstein Against the odds: The Great Quantum Debate."*

Science Digest, June 1983.

Jager, Melissa. Monograph: *"The Lamp Turn Laser."* of Monroe Institute

Applied Sciences, Faber, Va, undated.

Monroe, Robert A. *Journeys Out of the Body.* New York, Doubleday and Company, 1971.

Purce, Jill. *The Mystic Spiral.* New York, Thames and Hudson Inc., 1980.

Sannella, Lee., M.D., *Kundalini-Psychosis or Transcendence.* San Francisco, Henry S. Dakin, 1976.

(con't.)

Stone, Pat. *"Altered States of Consciousness"* The Mother Earth News,

March/April 1983.

Tart, Charles T. *Altered States of Consciousness.* New York, Wiley, 1969.

Original Report (CIA Electronic Reading Room)

The Hemi-Sync® Audios

SCIENCE

"Left Brain vs. Right Brain: What Does This Mean for Me?" (Healthline)

"Is Hypnosis Real" (Healthline)

"Meditation: In Depth" (NCCIH)

NEWS & OPINION

Binaural Beats & Hemi-Sync® (Motherboard — VICE)

The US Army Funded Astral Projection And Hypnosis Research in the '80s (Motherboard— VICE)

Additional Sources Sited

Wave I-VII audios and accompanying user manuals. The Monroe Institute.

www.CIA.gov. The Electronic Reading Room From the Freedom of Information Act. Various documents.

Table of Abbreviations

BST	Belief System Territory
CIA	Central Intelligence Agency
CPS	Cycles per Second
EBT	Energy Bar Tool
ECB	Energy Conversion Box
ELS	Earth Life System
FFR	Frequency Following Response
LBM	Living Body Map
NVC	Non-Verbal Communication
OBE	Out-of-body experience
REBAL	Resonant Energy Balloon
REM	Rapid eye movement

Made in United States
Troutdale, OR
06/13/2024

20557825R00236